Beth,
Your husband
had a great time
Mardi's funeral. That's
kinda weird —
love...

John Baker

Wild, Wonderful 'n Wacky

South Cackalacky

True Stories about Life in South Carolina

Compiled and Edited by

Sandy F. Richardson
and
Susan Doherty Osteen

Southern Sass Publishing Alliances

The stories in this collection are all true. In some instances, names of people and places have been changed to protect privacy. Some creative license has been taken in recreating conversations, and memory of order of events may differ slightly. Permission to print the lyrics of the state song is granted by Hank Martin.

Published by Southern Sass Publishing Alliances
Sumter, SC
www.SouthernSassPublishingAlliances.com

Praise for

Wild, Wonderful 'n Wacky
South Cackalacky
True Stories about Life in South Carolina

"Hold on tight as you take this ride through South Carolina, past and present. These writers find stories everywhere—from personal and family memories to the waiting room of a doctor's office. Whether it is a wild tale of a drunken date gone wrong or a warm memory of snapping speckled butter beans with grandma—disrupted by the intrusion of ghost story—you'll find yourself eagerly turning the pages for more."

-Kathryn Smith of Anderson is the author of *The Gatekeeper: Missy LeHand, FDR and the Untold Story of the Partnership that Defined a Presidency* and is co-author, with Kelly Durham, of *Shirley Temple Is Missing*. For information on her books, go to www.kathrynsmithwords.com

"These stories of family, old traditions and wild adventures illustrate the history of South Carolina and its people in a way that is real, visceral and, at times, laugh out loud funny. You'll see yourself, your friends and your relatives in these tall tales of childhood, growing up and growing old."

-Karen Dybis, author of *The Witch of Delray* and *Better Made in Michigan*

Praise for

Wild, Wonderful 'n Wacky
South Cackalacky

"We have all been in the company of cafe coffee-drinkers when someone tells a story, and it reminds someone else of something else, and that story is added to the heap, and another is told, then another, until the moment and the mood leaves us with a good and pleasing sensation. To me, these occasions are "Tellings." They happen in hundreds of thousands of places every day in every place on Earth where people gather. And so it is with this ambitious anthology, *Wild, Wonderful 'n Wacky, South Cackalacky: True Stories about Life in South Carolina,* fashioned by Sandy Richardson and Susan Doherty Osteen. The writers range in experience and in style, from simple memoir to creative hyperbole, but each offering is engaging and memorable. Read them with a cup of coffee, or a libation of your choice. You will swear you're in a familiar cafe with some talkative friends and being there, in that moment, is the only thing that matters."

-**Terry Kay**, a 2006 inductee into the Georgia Writers Hall of Fame, is the author of 17 published works, including *The King Who Made Paper Flowers*, *Song of the Vagabond Bird*, *The Greats of Cuttercane*, *Bogmeadow's Wish*, *The Book of Marie*, *To Dance with the White Dog*, *The Valley of Light*, *Taking Lottie Home*, *The Kidnapping of Aaron Greene*, *Shadow Song*, *The Runaway*, *Dark Thirty*, *After Eli*, and *The Year the Lights Came On*, as well as a book of essays, *Special K: The Wisdom of Terry Kay*, and two children's books, *The Seventh Mirror* and *To Whom the Angel Spoke*.

Praise for

Wild, Wonderful 'n Wacky
South Cackalacky

"Like Blues, Jazz, and Rock & Roll, great storytelling was born in the South. A region impoverished for most of its existence, the South has always been rich in creativity, individualism, and humor. In South Carolina, the gift of spinning a yarn has long been viewed as a gift on par with beauty, as it is the raconteur—not the belle of the ball—that draws the most attention. Within the pages of *Wild, Wonderful 'n Wacky, South Cackalacky*, you'll find the soul of South Carolina storytellers. No, not writers in the style of Faulkner or the prose of Conroy—these are the stories told on a veranda, or a picnic table, or on the front porch of a country store. Enjoy. I surely did."

-Prioleau Alexander, Author, *Dispatches Along the Way* and *You Want Fries With That?*

"South Carolina on My Mind"*

At the foot hills of the Appalachian chain,
Down through the rivers, to the coastal plain,
There's a place that I call home, and I'll never be alone,
Singin' this Carolina love song
I've got South Carolina on my mind
Remembering all those sunshine Summer times,
And the Autumns in the Smokies when the leaves turn to gold
touches my heart and thrills my soul
to have South Carolina on my mind,
With those clean snow-covered mountain Winter times
And the white sand of the beaches and those Carolina peaches,
I've got South Carolina on my mind.

I'm grown now with a family of my own
In a place that all my kids are callin' home.
And I love this life I'm livin', and thank God for all He's givin'
But my heart sings a Carolina love song
I've got South Carolina on my mind
Remembering all those sunshine Summer times,
And the Autumns in the Smokies when the leaves turn to gold
touches my heart and thrills my soul
to have South Carolina on my mind,
With those clean snow-covered mountain Winter times
And the white sand of the beaches and those Carolina peaches,
I've got South Carolina on my mind.

Written by Buzz Arledge and Hank Martin. Listen at
www.discogs.com/Hank-Martin-2-Buzz-Arledge-South-
Carolina-On-My-Mind/release/6996970.

*Adopted as the second state song by the SC Legislature in
1984. Lyrics used with permission by Hank Martin, 2018.

Dedication

This book is dedicated to the "smiling faces and beautiful places" of the state we love—

South Carolina.

Acknowledgements

Creating a book involves so much more than just the writing—although that alone is challenging in scope and detail. Several people offered special assistance, input, and support during the process of publishing *Wild, Wonderful 'n Wacky, South Cackalacky.*

We'd like to especially thank: our Sumter Critique Partners Peg Bell and Sherry Fasano, our supportive literary arts friends at USC Sumter, our loyal book seller and friend Betty Reese, and our special friends Lynn Alessandro, Lee Craig, Dr. J. Grady Locklear, Donny Floyd, and Ellen and Paul Vogel.

To our contributors: We thank you for sharing your wonderful stories, for your patience through all those revisions, and for your enthusiastic input all along the way.

And finally to our beloved husbands Phil and Jack and our amazing children Christy, Jay, Callison, Elise, and John: Thank you for always encouraging the pursuit of our dreams. We love you.

Sandy and Susan

Wild, Wonderful 'n Wacky
South Cackalacky

True Stories about Life in South Carolina

Table of Contents

Table of Contents

Table of Contents

Table of Contents

Introduction

The stories included here of everyday people living ordinary lives are as related to history as are the courageous armies, heroic battles, and glorified deeds we read of in other books. For the true who, what, when, why, and where of our existence are not found swathed in draped and pleated bunting or pinned with gold medals. Nor do parades herald them. Our REAL history is found in the keepsakes discovered in attic boxes or in conversations about the good or not-so-good days we've witnessed as individuals and as communities.

Real history is found in the stories we pass down generation to generation and friend to friend about the goings-on in everyday life. It has its beginnings in the conversations and memories of the old, and even in the young, as they share their lives with us.

History is in the high school yearbooks, the family Bibles, the lost and forgotten diaries of childhood, and the journals of the elderly. It is found in love letters brittle and yellow and tied with frayed, satin ribbons, in front-porch talk, in car-trip chatter. History—real history—is in the telling and retelling of our personal and collective stories.

The collection of essays, stories, and anecdotes in this anthology are a bit of that kind of history—pieces and parts of our lives as we have lived them in the state we love: South Carolina. They are family stories, stretched tales about people and places we knew or know, thoughtful considerations of past and present social issues, rambunctious tales of youth, and sobering thoughts about death and what lies beyond.

All these stories seek to record a truth and contribute something of personal value to the historical record of the wild, wonderful, and wacky place we call home: South Carolina.

We hope you enjoy them.

Sandy Richardson and Susan Doherty Osteen

A Carpetbagger's Tale

Pat Willer

The first things I bought for our new home were cleaning supplies from the neighborhood Winn Dixie. It was our first full day as residents of Columbia, and we had all of two days to prepare the empty house for our worldly goods which were following us by moving van from Kansas. The grocery cart was piled high with mop and broom and a bucket for mixing dangerous chemicals.

The first thing I didn't buy was the large Mason jar on the bottom shelf that my son pointed to with some trepidation.

"What is that?" Robb asked. I looked and looked away.

"I don't think we need to know."

"Really, Mom, what is it?"

As a precaution, we both moved to the far side of the aisle, the metal cart between us and the strangely pink, oozy flesh color emanating from inside the glass. They looked like large, distended, chopped off thumbs, harvested from giants. I swear I saw them move. The label read:

Herb's Pickled Pigs' Feet

Our Feet Can't Be Beat

We fled with our cart through the checkout line and raced to our car.

Thus began our southern sojourn, a stopover that lasted more than twenty years. And, like so many Northerners before us, we began to realize that we had, indeed, moved to a land far, far away.

My husband and I had positions at the University, and we were mostly focused on getting those new jobs right. Our eleven year old started middle school two weeks after our arrival and his was a total immersion experience. Robb was excited to be invited to a friend's slumber party but came home tired (not unusual, since nobody ever sleeps at a good sleep over) and cranky.

After some prodding, he explained that his friend's mother had appeared that morning with a perky manner and an offer to make grits for those that wanted them. Robb responded to this as the joke he thought it was. But while he was making a face, all the other boys waved their hands and shouted. "Me! Me! Me!" Robb was out of sync and hungry. It took a trip to the Rosewood Dairy Bar to make things right.

But he hung in there. Most afternoons, I came home from work to find him in our back yard, playing catch by throwing a tennis ball against the side of the garage wall. This was his way of decompressing, and he could throw that ball for hours. I found the rhythmic thump, thump, thump to be soothing, but I wondered if our neighbors did. The families next door on both sides had kids, so I figured the noise would not be an issue. I wasn't so sure that the elderly widow lady behind us would appreciate it. But in fact, it was quite the opposite. Robb and Miss Parrott began having neighborly conversations over the fence while he tossed and caught the ball, and she, dressed in sun hat and gardening gloves, delicately snipped spent flowers from her Lady Banksia rose bushes.

One night Robb came into the kitchen after playing outside, grabbed the milk bottle from the fridge and poured himself a tall one.

"Mom, I've got something I need to tell you." As any mother knows, this is never a good start to a conversation.

"Okay," I responded with a question in my voice and put down the spatula. Ready for anything.

"We're Presbyterians."

I guess I wasn't ready for anything. Certainly not that.

"What do you mean, we're Presbyterians? Honey, we're not anything. We're not religious. You know that."

"But Miss Parrott keeps asking me what we are. I had to tell her something."

I shook my head. "Why Presbyterian? You can't even spell Presbyterian. Hell, I can't even spell Presbyterian. And I don't think there are very many around here."

My son looked at me like I was missing some I.Q. points.

"That's why it's perfect. I couldn't tell her Baptist. She would just want to know which church we joined. No one is Presbyterian."

Religion. It was an issue I had encountered at work. After all, there were so many churches in town people called it Columbia, the Gem of Devotion. I had received so many invitations from colleagues at work eager to share their church with me that I had begun to wonder if they got finder fees for lassoing fresh ones into their congregations.

"I just tell people I was raised Catholic. That usually settles it. Nobody expects an ex-Catholic to become a Baptist."

"Won't work for me, Mom. I've only been to church once with Grandma, and I don't think Dad liked it. Besides," he added. "It's not just Miss Parrott. Kids at school ask, too, even the cool ones. Last week we worked on costumes for the play in English. All the boys are supposed to pull their sweat socks up to their knees over their pant legs to make them look old-timey. And wear suit coats."

"That sounds good."

"Mom, I don't have a suit coat! And when I said that in class, Jackson asked me what I wore to church. I said we didn't wear suits to church in Kansas, but nobody believed me."

The next day, we got a nice tweed sports coat at the second hand store. And, no, we did not become Presbyterians.

But we did persevere. It took me two months, but I finally got the hang of the "Hey" greeting. As a new employee, I was eager to please my boss, who I mainly encountered in the hall, and usually when he was rushing to a meeting. Our conversations tended along these lines.

"Hey," he'd say, striding fast while shuffling papers.

"Yes?" I would respond, stopping in the hall.

"Yes, what?" he would ask, stopping as well.

"I thought you wanted something," I would explain.

"Uh, no." He would push his glasses further up his nose and check his watch.

And so it would go until I finally captured the meaning of "Hey" and quit accosting the poor man as he ran late to his meetings. Just say "Hello," and keep moving. That was the key.

Of course, by that time, I had been adopted by a lovely lady who was determined to help an outsider navigate her beloved South. Miss Betty was a retired librarian and the president of a community group that provided hospitality and support to the University's international students. She must have seen me as a confused foreigner suffering from culture shock. She had it about right.

First she cleared up the matter of the churches. We had several Baptist churches in my hometown in Kansas, but only one was Southern Baptist. I had expected to find many more in the South. Why else would they call them Southern Baptist? So I asked Miss Betty why there weren't more.

She looked puzzled.

"Why, Pat," she explained. "They are <u>all</u> Southern Baptist churches. We don't have that other kind." Case closed.

And then there was the matter of the crustless cucumber sandwiches. Miss Betty had invited me to join the board of her community group. I attended every meeting dutifully and could even make a constructive comment upon occasion. At least I could up until the day we discussed the menu for the annual tea party.

The tea party was a lovely affair held each spring on the grounds of the Governor's mansion for international students from across the state. Students arrived by the busloads and were quickly hustled through the Governor's Mansion tour and out to the fabulous garden, alive with flowering azaleas and dogwood trees in full bloom.

In the garden, the ladies of the organization arranged tables full of Southern delicacies: tea sandwiches, cheese straws and an amazing array of homemade cookies. Sweet tea and pink lemonade were the beverages of choice.

Planning for all this took months of work. I was no stranger to event planning, but the attention to detail by the tea party delegation was truly phenomenal. Why, one whole board meeting was devoted to the specifications of the cucumber sandwiches. It appeared there had been some controversy the previous year when some of the ladies preparing sandwiches had neglected to produce crustless triangles of cucumber and cream cheese.

The board was divided. Some felt that a truly elegant tea party that reflected well on Southern traditions required that crusts be removed. Others thought that practice a waste of good food. The discussion took a turn for the worse when the word "tacky" was uttered.

Miss Betty suggested a brief intermission.

Out in the hallway she pulled me aside. "Nobody's going to say it, but what they are really arguing about is Low Country versus Country."

I knew Low Country meant Charleston, the oldest and most status conscious part of the state.

"So Low Country is crustless?" I guessed.

Miss Betty nodded. "Country people grew up having less and don't believe in wasting food. And," she added, "They don't much like being looked down upon."

The meeting resumed, and Miss Betty made an executive decision. That year they would do fifty per cent with crusts and fifty per cent without. That seemed fair to everyone, and the matter was closed.

Or almost closed. One newcomer to the board, obviously a health nut, commented that she liked to make her cucumber sandwiches with whole wheat bread.

"Much healthier," she noted.

"No, dear," said Miss Betty. "This meeting is adjourned."

Some months later, Miss Betty and I attended a conference in another state. To keep our expenses down, we chose to share a hotel room.

After a long day of meetings, we headed to the hotel bar. Miss Betty did not herself imbibe, but was good company nonetheless and didn't even raise an eyebrow when I ordered a second gin and tonic. She told funny stories about Southern belles, including one about how important it was to have real pearls, not fakes. She was, of course, wearing real ones while telling the tale. The two of us had a lovely time. Then we toddled off to bed.

I changed into a sleep shirt and snuggled under the covers. A few moments later, Miss Betty emerged from the bathroom. She wore a blue striped cotton seersucker dressing gown. Peeking from underneath the lacy collar was a strand of pearls. Her real ones.

"My God, Betty, you people even wear pearls to bed," I gasped.

"Oh, my, yes," she answered. "But we don't do the pill box hat or white gloves anymore." With that, she turned off the light.

At Christmas time that year, Betty and I exchanged gifts. As I recall, my present for her was something eminently suitable for a retired librarian, probably stationary. But she surprised me yet again. Nestled in my gift bag, as if in waiting to educate me further, lay a book, *A Southern Belle Primer: Why Princess Margaret Will Never Be a Kappa Gamma.*

And, yes, there was a section on pearls.

Carolina Afternoons

Sherry Fasano

Robins twittered around the yard as I pumped my legs back and forth, my bare toes almost reaching the tops of the pines. Nanny, our elderly neighbor and my babysitter, relaxed in a metal yard chair with her eyes closed. She hummed while fanning her face with a cardboard fan.

A busy morning—we began right after breakfast moving root-bound plants that wintered in the flower house to long wooden tables in the backyard. As Nanny loaded a rusty wagon as full as it could get for one trip after another, I plundered underneath shelves through lamb shaped planters and pastel vases tangled in spider webs. The morning of hard work suited me just fine. The smell of warm dirt and leaves stretching toward the sun signaled the beginning of summer.

DeeDee, a gentle collie who had been around longer than I, plopped down by Nanny's chair and whined.

"I think he misses Spot, Nanny. Where is she, today?"

Opening one eye, Nanny reached over and patted DeeDee's head. "Spot's in jail this week, Miss Priss. We can't risk her getting into trouble again."

Spot, who looked like a black and white sausage on short legs, had a hard time staying out of trouble. Every so often during any given year, Nanny shooed Spot into a big dog house and pushed a wire gate against the opening, and DeeDee whined until Spot was free again.

The loud clang of a hammer hitting metal interrupted any further questions from me about Spot's punishment.

"Goose-Paw's at it again, Nanny. Wonder what he's building today?"

"Never can tell." She winked. "He's always puttering away at something."

Just then, a burst of blue and yellow sparks showered out of the window of Goose-Paw's shop across the road. I knew I ought to turn my head away because he often warned of the dangers of watching the fire from his welding machine, but the sparkles reminded me of the Fourth of July, and I peeked in spite of myself.

Sometimes, for profit, he used bits and pieces he brought home from his salvage business. The oddest things came home in the back of his truck, and he piled them in the field across the road. Clawfoot tubs and old toilets sat between rows of faded window sashes and stacks of tall doors. Mama

said the view from our front windows sure would improve if
Goose-Paw cleared the junk or just let wisteria and kudzu vines
grow over it. Sometimes Daddy argued with him about the mess
across from our house, but Goose-Paw never paid any mind to
his complaints. And actually, I thought the junk held lots of
possibilities.

One summer day, Goose-Paw drove up in his old dump
truck with a big smile on his face and the skeleton of a huge
swing set in the bed of the truck. My excitement grew with each
piece he welded together. Soon three swings, a see-saw, and a
sliding board rose in the side yard of their house. I learned if I
rubbed the shiny silver slide with pine straw I could zip down
it fast as lightning.

After that, the side yard became the spot where Nanny
and I usually ended up at the end of the day. Nanny puttered in
flowerbeds or sat in the metal chairs scratching the dogs behind
their ears while I climbed the sliding board again and again.

Once a week, the preacher's shiny car pulled into the
driveway. He walked across the yard kind of stiff legged with a
smile stretched out on his face.

"Afternoon, Sister Mary. Flowers are looking mighty
fine. Is Brother Miles around?"

On those days, Nanny used her special company voice
when she called out to Goose-Paw, "Miles, Brother Alton's
here!"

Goose-Paw, smelling like hard work, hurried from his shop right away because he held the preacher in high regard.

Sometimes Brother Alton sat in a metal yard chair and shot the breeze with Goose-Paw, laughing and calling out a lot of loud "Amens" as they talked. Other times, he stood by the car and asked things like, "Brother Miles, you s'pose you could stop by the church tomorrow and fix that leaking toilet in the Men's Room? And while you're there, you might check the sagging door in the vestibule. That would be fine if you would, yes sir, just fine."

Goose-Paw, a willing worker, always agreed. One day he even granted one favor to the preacher that had nothing at all to do with fixing something. And I'll never forget it.

Shortly after one of Brother Alton's visits, I noticed a lot of comings and goings out behind the wash house. A tall metal trash barrel appeared back there, and Nanny visited it every day after lunch. On each trip out there, she toted a metal pail. When I asked her about it she said, "Just never you mind."

But I did mind, and I kept asking until I learned the truth. Brother Alton wanted to bake a possum, and Goose-Paw had found him one. It scratched in the bottom of that barrel. After that, I followed Nanny out there to feed him every day, but the sound of the scared little critter scurrying round and round inside the barrel made me sad.

Then it occurred to me the possum would make a good pet. And she already knew one trick, playing dead.

I named her Donna. I watched her grow fatter and fatter and tried my best to convince Nanny and Goose-Paw I could tame her, but they paid me no mind. In the end, my tearful pleas to spare the beady-eyed, hissing critter made no difference.

The same afternoon Brother Alton left with Donna in the bottom of a burlap bag, Nanny took my hand, and we walked to the wash house. In the back corner, Nanny bent low and pointed behind the washing machine. There squirmed a brand new litter of black kittens.

"Must've been born last night, Miss Priss. They're all gonna need names, and I'll just bet there's a 'Donna' somewhere in the bunch."

"C-c-can we re-re-really keep 'em, Nanny?"

Nanny pulled a handkerchief out of her pocket and dried my tears. "I probably just traded a devil for a witch," she smiled, "But I s'pose so."

The kittens eased my sadness, but I still refused meat at Nanny and Goose-Paw's table and from that day on I never smiled at Brother Alton, even when he smiled at me.

Several weeks passed, and the possum memory seemed a long time ago as I pulled against the swing chains and pumped my legs. Honeysuckle bloomed on old bathtubs and window sashes across the road, and the air smelled sweet. I closed my eyes and drew a deep breath. The screened door creaked open, scattering a few of the Donna's playing on the back steps into a hydrangea bush. Nanny waved as she stepped off the porch carrying cold RC Colas and Moon Pies.

"Hey Miss Priss, you think you could take a little break before you end up in the clouds?"

I pumped hard one more time, stretching my toes toward the Carolina blue sky. Then I dragged my feet through the powdery sand, slowing the swing. I grinned.

"Betcha I can beat ya to the picnic table, Nanny!"

Nanny grinned back, and we both took off running.

Believe!

Sandy Richardson

It was the summer of '66 just before our first year of high school. We thought we knew everything. But actually, we were clueless—about life, the world, and what really mattered. Still we were young. We were sassy. And we had great skin—well, except for the occasional pimple that usually appeared on the night before any big event in our sheltered lives.

Having good skin mattered so much back then because of the associations made between our skin and our social standing. Those associations could make or break a girl in high school circles. "They," the classmates who arbitrarily made decisions on our popularity, based our entrance into their social circle on cuteness, hair, clothes, boyfriends, and, of course, skin. Even wealth and heritage, those long-time, Southern, guaranteed-acceptance norms, could not overcome those particular high school ratings.

I once had a boyfriend who flirted with another girl because she had beautiful skin. "Why do you have to have all those freckles," he asked me.

He later apologized—but too late—damage done. For a long time afterward, I viewed my light sprinkle of nose-freckles as heinous and totally gross in comparison to her naturally beautiful complexion.

But at least I didn't have acne, or worse—warts. My friend Nancy had warts. Not the huge, single, seedy warts that popped up on children's hands every summer—the ones caused by frogs peeing on you, or so we were told. Instead, my friend's warts grew in small, flesh-colored patches. Patches that popped up on her hands, her arms, her neck, and even on her face.

Of course, for any fifteen-year-old girl, those almost-invisible warts, like my faint freckles, might as well have been raisins splattering her body. Nancy grew increasingly self-conscious about them.

In efforts to hide or camouflage the scourge, she took to wearing high collared, long sleeved blouses year round. (And in South Carolina summers that was akin to living in hell's fire and brimstone.) She also piled on thick, pancake makeup that promised to hide even the worst blotches, but, of course, did not. And most often, she kept her hands in her pockets whenever she could.

But, of course, none of this worked to solve the real problem.

Nancy had seen several doctors about the condition. Each doctor prescribed a different torture. There were peeling lotions, skin burnings, and wart cuttings. Add to those, pills and scrapings, all to no avail. The warts always came back.

So, that summer before entering high school, Nancy was desperate for a solution.

Late one afternoon, the three of us drove out beyond the city limits and turned down a sandy, rutted road—not much more than a trail, actually. We bumped along beneath a canopy of oaks and Spanish moss, crossing eventually into the cool dimness of a pine woods. Rabbits, deer, and squirrels darted for cover as deeper and deeper into the darkness we traveled.

"Now, girls," Nancy's mom said. "I want you to promise you won't breathe a word of what is about to happen to anyone. This is our secret, okay?"

Nancy and I nodded obediently, but continued to sneak questioning, side-ways glances at each other. We had no idea where she was taking us or what was about to happen. All she had said was, "We're going on a mission."

Back then, eye-rolling had not been thought of as a way to express feelings; instead, we grew very adept at arching one eyebrow, an expression inspired by the big-screen movie actresses at the time. Scarlett, herself, was particularly good at the expression.

"Hang on Sloopy" blasted from the rear speakers of the car as Mrs. Norman navigated the rutted road. With seat belts not yet mandatory in cars, Nancy and I hung on to the armrests as we bounced along.

Then Mrs. Norman made a sharp turn into blinding sunlight and a huge field of corn. The whole scene made me think of Tennyson's poem, "The Charge of the Light Brigade." I even caught myself muttering, "Corn to the right of me, Corn to the left of me, Corn in front of me."

Nancy giggled from her corner.

Years later, I watched the movie *Children of the Corn* and thought back on that trip, happy I had not seen the movie before that particular day.

Mrs. Norman reached for the radio knob and after a few seconds of loud static, Eddy Arnold's deep voice begged us to "Make the World Go Away." The "crying music," as Nancy and I called it, lulled my thoughts of poems of war with its aching sadness.

Soon the humidity rose so high in the car, my head felt groggy. I caught myself dozing several times as the drive continued.

Sometime later—could have been five minutes, could have been 50—my body shifted as the car took a sharp right turn, and my head jerked up when the car bounced Nancy and me in the back seat. I scrubbed at my sweaty face and looked up just as Mrs. Norman stopped short in front of a ramshackle cabin trimmed in "haint blue" paint. Three tow-headed children, two goats, and a number of chickens scattered at our arrival.

Mrs. Norman cut the engine. Nancy and I gawked.

To the side of the house, a huge black iron pot smoldered in the afternoon sun. A noxious smell followed the streams of smoke and filled the air. On the porch, various dried, plant bundles hung across the eaves. Skulls of what looked like small animals and even one of a cow lined the railing. A woman and a man, both wrinkled and burnt by the sun, rocked in the shadows of the porch shade.

"Everybody out!" Mrs. Norman said, sounding downright giddy.

"Mama, what is this place? What are we doing here?"

"We're here to rid you of warts, Nancy-my-girl."

"Huh?"

"Move. Let's go," Mrs. Norman replied.

"But who are those people?"

Mrs. Norman turned to glare at her daughter. "Don't be rude. It's none of your business what their names are. Now out."

We scooted out of the car, but stood ready to dive back in. Nancy punched her elbow into my side. I chewed on my bottom lip, trying to take in the strangeness of the little cabin, the isolation, and the bent, old man now standing at the top of his porch steps. He motioned for us to come up.

Still, Nancy and I hesitated. Mrs. Norman made her way up to the porch and leaned in close to the man to whisper in his ear. He, in turn, nodded his head and patted Mrs. Norman's shoulder, while she nodded towards the other woman. Mrs. Norman walked to the other end of the porch and perched against the railing there. The old man stared in our directions. He snapped his fingers, pointed at us and then to his porch.

Nancy and I stumbled forward. "Oh God! She's brought us to the root-doctor," Nancy whispered. "I've heard about him and his wife. They work all kinds of magic spells for people. Their children go to school with my brother, and he's always talking about the peculiar things they sometimes bring to school in little bags for the teacher."

I swallowed, dry-mouthed.

The man motioned again, more impatiently, and we stumbled up the wooden steps to the porch.

By that time, the woman had walked forward. Neither she nor the man spoke, but she pointed toward two small stools, one by the railing, the other in front of the rocker where the old man had been sitting when we first arrived. I pushed Nancy aside and took the stool by the rail. I wasn't the one with warts, after all.

We took our seats, Nancy gnawing at her thumbnail, me, crossing my arms and pressing my hands in my armpits. The man opened the creaky screened door, and he and the woman disappeared into the darkness inside the house.

"Mama?"

"Shhhhh! Just do whatever he says do."

One look at Nancy's pale face told me her insides jittered around just like mine. "What's he gonna do…" Her lips closed around the rest of her words as the man returned to the porch holding a red-velvet pouch that shined like a ruby in the dim porch light. He lowered himself into his chair in front of her and grunted.

I stared at his knobby fingers struggling with the cord on the pouch and pulling the mouth of the bag wide. Then, he pulled the opening up to cover his mouth and began to murmur a strange pulsing melody that enveloped us in the quiet shade of the porch. I couldn't make out specific words, but he was definitely singing or humming or …conjuring.

Without a beat missed, he lowered the bag, and his fingers dove into the pouch and pulled up a mess of dried bits that looked like crumbled leaves. I swear I saw snakeskins in there, too.

The man snapped the strings tight around the top of the pouch and laid the pouch to his side. When he finally turned to look at Nancy, it was clear he wasn't really seeing her. His eyes glowed white as a full moon, whether from age or disease, I didn't know, but he definitely couldn't see.

"Gimme a new quarter. Quick," the man said, stretching out his hand towards Mrs. Norman. She rummaged around in her purse, pulled out a white bank envelope, and trip-trapped in her high-heels across the porch to pour the shiny coin into his hand.

The man reached out and took Nancy's hand in his. Shocked at his sudden movement, we both sucked in a gulp of air. He carefully pushed up the long sleeve of Nancy's blouse and began a slow and careful massage of the warts on her arm and down to her hand farther down to each finger, rubbing both the quarter and the dried bits from his bag in circles over each patch of warts. He mumbled or hummed—maybe he chanted, and while he did this, his white eyeballs twitched in their sockets. And from inside the house, I heard the woman's voice join in harmony with his.

Next he pushed aside Nancy's high collar and with a hand on each side of her neck, he repeated the same slow, steady circular motions across her face and even up to the top of her head. Nancy had closed her eyes, but I watched as her head nodded back and forth with the rhythm of his words.

The heat, the sickly-sweet smoke from the fire out front, the rise and fall of the chanting, all created some sort of cocoon, locking the four of us on that porch, all of us swaying without meaning to, as the chant continued.

Then, it stopped. Like someone had lifted the needle of a phonograph.

The man slapped his hands together in front of Nancy's face and shouted, "Believe!"

I nearly jumped right off that porch. Nancy's stool tilted sideways spilling her to the floor, but the man caught her and pulled her up and steadied her back in her seat. He took her right hand and stared directly into her face. "Nev'ah speak of yo' time here, gal."

He pressed the quarter firmly into her palm. "Take this home. Hide it special. Where no one knows." He glanced over at me and then turned back to Nancy. "Hide it, and never go back. Warts be gone. Believe!"

He gently closed Nancy's fingers around the quarter. Then he sat back in his rocker, closed his eyes, and sighed.

The woman came out to the porch, swiping her hands down the sides of her dress. Without a word, Mrs. Norman walked up to the woman and placed another white envelope in her palm. Then she hustled Nancy and me to the car.

When we settled in, Mrs. Norman turned to face us. "You two need to forget all about what happened here, you hear me? Won't do to go talking this all over town. Bad for them, and bad for us."

She sped out of the yard stirring up dust clouds and almost hitting a strutting rooster in our escape. She jerked the wheel sharply to avoid it, and my head bumped the side window. I struggled to pull myself up straight in the seat, aching with the same kind of heaviness I felt when I woke from a long nap on a hot summer day. When I tried in my mind to grab hold of what had happened, the sounds, the smells, even the people we had seen furred around the edges.

Next to me, Nancy slept, crimped against the car door. I glanced out of the rear window. The cabin with the blue shutters was no longer there—only the dust blowing behind us into the tight rows of corn and the dripping moss that grabbed at the car as it crept along beneath the scattered oaks—just as if I had fallen asleep and dreamed of conjurers and spells and white-haired children.

Mrs. Norman pulled into her driveway and shut off the engine. Nancy opened the rear door and with her fist clenched, she raced into the yard, disappearing behind the spirea hedge.

From there, she could have gone most anywhere: into the outdoor shed, to the vegetable garden, even far into the woods that bordered the property. She came back a while later, but I never asked where she had gone. She wouldn't have told me anyway. One thing I do know: she came back empty-handed.

A week later, Nancy's warts vanished.

We never talked about the day the root doctor cured her. But I thought of it recently and wanted to make sure it wasn't just a dream. And so I asked, "Have you ever gone back to find that quarter the root doctor gave you?"

Nancy didn't answer. She drew close, rolled her eyes back in their sockets, and leaned toward me.

"Believe!" she shouted and held out her aged, but wart-free hands.

The Tonsillectomy

David F. McInnis, Sr.

Most memories I have from the age of four are very good and point to a happy childhood. But there was one exception.

Sometime during my fourth year, my mother broke the news that I was going to undergo a very exciting experience. My tonsils and adenoids would be removed to prevent the sore throats and sinus problems that had plagued my young life. But she neglected to mention I was also to be circumcised at the same time.

Today's modern medical advice prescribes that male children be circumcised shortly after birth, and I am now a strong supporter of this theory. But that was not always the conventional wisdom.

Haunting me still are the terrible smell of ether and the feeling of suffocation as I was being anesthetized in Dr. Davenport's office above the drug store on Main St.

in Timmonsville, South Carolina. And to add pain to misery, the ether made me nauseated when I woke up from the surgery.

Now, even at that tender age, I knew that having tonsils removed created some pain and discomfort for a day or two because I had observed other family members and neighborhood children recovering from tonsil surgery. And I was prepared to endure the discomfort while enjoying a constant supply of ice cream, which was prescribed to ease the pain in my throat.

I was not prepared, however, for the pain in other areas of my body that no amount of ice cream seemed to ease. I simply could not figure out what having your tonsils removed had to do with the pain I was suffering elsewhere because the area of pain was nowhere close to my throat.

A day or two into the recovery process, I also became aware of the difference in appearance in that foreign part of my anatomy. The end of my penis looked like someone had attached a number of black spiders to it. These "spiders" were actually black stitches.

Furthermore, at that time in medical practices, there were no ultra violet lights for use in the healing process. At least, there were none in Timmonsville. The doctor advised my mother to sit me out in the yard with no clothes on below my waist and to place my wounded member directly in the sun. This would allow me to soak up the healing ultra violet light rays of the sun.

This practice, which my mother strictly adhered to, proved to offer a number of embarrassing incidents. Day after day, she sat me in a recliner facing Hwy. 76, which ran in front of our house and about 30 feet away. One of the few sidewalks in town also ran in front of our house beside that highway.

My best friend and next door neighbor at the time was Dickey Knopf, also four years old. Dickey remained my constant companion for the first three days of my "airing" and took great pride in "showing off" his best friend and explaining my predicament to every little girl between the ages of three and six years old in Timmonsville.

So by the third day of treatment, I was a city landmark. The foot traffic in front of our house picked up four-fold during those few days. Even adults abandoned their cars to walk a few blocks to witness the phenom.

Thankfully, my father finally convinced my mother that the sun's rays shone just as strong in the back yard as the front, and so my recliner and I were mercifully moved away from the eyes of the public. Dickey was crushed to move out of the limelight, but I was delighted.

Further, I have often thought that if I ever suffer any serious mental illness that can be traced to my childhood, one need look no farther than those few days in 1938 when humiliation became a daily expense.

Ghosts on Golf Carts

Susan Doherty Osteen

On Daufuskie Island, the most southern of South Carolina's sea islands, I was given a small bead, a circular trinket of white, on which I noted a curious blue orb trapped in an unsettling black bull's eye.

"To chase away evil spirits," Roger told me. I smiled at him, as though we were sharing an inside joke. He didn't smile back. "Keep it in your pocket while you are on the island."

I examined the gift, rolling the round bead between my forefinger and thumb. The tiny eye and I stared back at each other with suspicion.

"Um, thanks," I muttered, hoping to sound sincere, but sounding quite skeptical to my own ears. Roger smiled at my response, but the look implied pity rather than humor. I put the glass bead in my pocket and forgot it.

Daufuskie is an unconventional haven. No bridge connects this island to the mainland, and temperamental tides and ocean currents distort her relative proximity to Hilton Head, South Carolina and Savannah, Georgia. Daufuskie is accessible only by boat.

Cars do not make sense on this small Banana Republic. They must be shipped in by barge and gas sells for a premium at the marina. Most people choose to get from one end of the island to the other by golf cart, a simple mode of transport requiring complex math. For an island outing one must factor in a maximum speed of five miles per hour. The island is only eight square miles, but on foot or on golf cart Daufuskie is quite a formidable territory to cover.

Remnants of Gullah houses dot the unpaved and unmarked roads. The small hipped-roof structures housed the descendants of slaves, people who stayed on Daufuskie to work the fabled oyster industry. Gullah stories and legends season the local population and fan tourism business. But even though the Geechee, as they are also known, are disappearing into memory and folklore, their supernatural spirits still have a tight grip on Daufuskie.

My tour guide Roger had agreed to properly introduce me to the island. He tried to weave the essence of this strange island into an understandable story for a *Comeya*, or newcomer to the island. This is opposed to a *Beenya*, a local. His version of Daufuskie, highly peppered with personal anecdotes and tall tales, was complicated by the constant bump, bump, bump of the golf cart over dirt roads and sandy beaches. My tour proved fascinating, but it did not strike me as paranormal. I forgot the small glass trinket he gave me. The eye hid deep in my jean pocket, eventually lost or eaten by my washing machine.

On subsequent visits to the island, I traveled with my accomplice and photographer, Donny. We wanted to chronicle the island, I through words, and Donny through pictures. I argue Donny found the ghost. Donny claims the haunting was my fault for ignoring Roger's advice and losing my good luck charm.

Our golf cart was new and electric, kept in tip-top service by mechanics at the Mansion at Haig Point, our residence for the adventure. Donny and I drove our cart to Bloody Point and spent the morning photographing the slave cemetery. The beach's morbid moniker tells of three deadly battles between the colonists and the Native Americans during the Yemassee War. In modern day, the most frightening aspect about Bloody Point is the tide that threatens to wash away the graves. If a headstone rests on nothing but a sharp drop into the Atlantic, reason follows that one of the souls buried facing east has taken a few steps closer home.

Donny snapped shots of the handmade tombstones and the twisted, bleached bones of beach wood. Bloody Point sounds haunted. But this is not where we first encountered the ghost.

We picked up the ghost *after* lunch.

I remember that meal, not so much because it was the last thing I ate before the haunting, but because it was absolutely delicious – the first time I ever ate a fried baloney sandwich.

"The key is to get good baloney, slice it thick, and grill it in butter," said Craig, the cook at the only island restaurant serving lunch, the Freeport Marina. "You want to get a little sear on it. Then add a just-sliced homegrown tomato. The tomato's got to be warm ... just picked off the vine. Then you put a little mayo and crisp lettuce on white bread. Man! It doesn't get better."

Craig spoke the gospel truth, so we listened carefully when he suggested a venue for an afternoon field trip.

"You guys need to check out the old Oyster House," he said. We were too consumed with fresh tomato dripping from the sides of our mouths to reply, but we nodded in agreement. Our golf cart was three-quarters fully charged, so even with Craig's hazy directions we figured we had plenty of juice to drive across the island. We did not figure on the ghost.

The Oyster House is the only two-story Gullah structure on the island. Donny and I had crisscrossed the island via golf cart dozens of times but never stumbled upon the abandoned building deep in the maritime forest. The rickety roof, leaning walls, and broken panes of glass provided the perfect setting for a horror film. But at the time, my fear stemmed from snakes. I could not actually see them, but the decades of fallen leaves and pine straw, the too-quiet, open crawlspace under the house, and the knee-high brambles around the door suggested them. My mind's eye kept returning to the copperhead we saw earlier that morning, flattening its rust-colored body as we rolled by on the cart.

"If I were a snake, this is where I would live," Donny said as he read my thoughts.

Gingerly, we began to pick our way closer and closer. My heart sounded loudly in my ears, and my boots shook with each step. Then, without warning, a hand grabbed the back of my neck.

I was too frightened and surprised to verbalize a single syllable. Wheeling round to face my attacker, I saw Donny pinching a raisin-sized mass between his thumb and forefinger.

"Look at this monster," he said, holding out a mammoth deer tick. "It was on your neck." I waded back through the brush to the golf cart and fortified with an entire can of Deep Woods OFF.™

I returned to find the house had swallowed my friend. The only door to the building was missing, either decayed or stolen to recycle in another dwelling. I wondered if I were brave enough to step through the entrance and execute a search and rescue.

"Wow!" I heard him say from somewhere inside.

Like a scripted cartoon character, I slowly poked my head into the house. My eyes took several seconds to adjust to the dimness. I saw a forgotten room, a meeting hall crumbling away beneath the elements, benches torn apart by animals, or maybe the weather, paint worn off the wall, trees moving in through busted windows, and a dilapidated staircase rising up to darkness.

"I'm going upstairs to take pictures," Donny said.

"Don't you dare," I whispered.

I was not afraid of ghosts. At that moment I still did not believe in ghosts. But I did believe in coyotes, rabid squirrel, snakes, and man-eating ticks. I also believed in alligators, and although the chance was slim that an alligator would be hiding upstairs, I had seen so many on the island I was not ruling them out. My only defense weapon was my ballpoint pen.

"I'm going up. Are you coming?" Donny said.

"No," I said firmly.

He went upstairs with his Nikon. "Wow!" I heard him say again. "I'm going to shoot this in panoramic mode. You need to see this."

All I could hear was the click-swish, click-swish of the shutter snapping. I held my breath and searched the ground for snakes. Finally, I heard Donny's boots coming down the stairs, and I sighed with relief. His red hair popped through the doorway, and we were a team again.

"I want to get a close up of the weathered wood," he said as he zoomed in on the wall of the house. He focused the lens. Nothing happened. His camera seemed to be stuck. He tried, again and again, flipping buttons and settings, but the camera would not cooperate.

Then we heard three loud knocks from inside the wall. Donny turned the color of a hardboiled egg.

"What was that?" he asked.

"A squirrel … or a possum… some small animal trapped between the walls," I offered.

"Susan," he said through tight lips. "Look inside again."

For the second time, I cautiously poked my head into the dark interior of the Oyster House and immediately saw the flaw in my logic. Flecks of filtered sunlight seeped through cracks in the single layer of wooden planks. *There was no inside wall.*

"Let's get out of here," Donny said. I was all too happy to agree. The fact we had not encountered a single snake was a true miracle. We hopped through bush and bramble back to the golf cart. Donny took the break off and turned the key.

Nothing.

He tried again. Nothing.

The battery level was mysteriously on empty. I could tell he was muttering some sort of a prayer as he turned the key a third time. This brought the golf cart back to life, but the needle hovered over "E."

"That," he said as we bumped down the dirt path. "Was a haint."

I laughed. I did not believe in ghosts. But I also did not believe we would make it back to Haig Point in a golf cart dangerously low on battery power. We willed our four wheels to take us a few hundred yards to the first house we knew, a Gullah shack-turned-art gallery owned by our friend Jack.

As we walked through the door, Donny announced we had picked up a ghost at the old Oyster House. I expected Jack to laugh, but instead he frowned and raised his eyebrows.

Donny began sputtering out the story, from tick to dead golf cart. Color returned to his face, now eggplant in hue, and I was much more worried he would have a heart attack than I was about a supernatural spirit.

"What you have," Jack said in a matter-of-fact tone as he plugged our golf cart into the outlet in his work shed, "Is a haint."

Donny shot me a knowing look.

Jack began to tell stories about haints, hags, and witch doctors from his boyhood. He grew up on Tybee, a Georgia sea island visible from the Savannah River side of Daufuskie. Gullah culture, with its mysterious tales, dialect, and magic, was very real to Jack.

Haints, according to Jack, were meddlesome ghosts. They generally can't hurt their victims directly. Instead, they disrupt radio waves, turn over pots, make noise, and steal electricity.

Hags, or boo hags as they are often called, are much more sinister. These evil creatures are more vampire than ghost, feeding on breath instead of blood. At night they discard their skin and slip through the smallest keyhole or crack, searching for victims. Borrowing breath is called "riding," and the hags will ride someone until dawn when they must return to their skin or be destroyed by the light.

"Hags will latch on and ride you to the death," Jack warned. "If a hag gets hold of you, she might never let go."

There are some preventative measures to keep spirits away. The easiest is to embrace blue. "Haint Blue," specifically. Unless conveyed by a boat, haints and hags are unable to cross water, which they associate with the color blue. The Gullah people paint windows, doors, thresholds, and entire houses bright aqua to keep away spirits.

If only we had driven a blue golf cart.

Jack and Donny discussed other preventive measures for ghosts: bottle trees, brooms, sieves, hocus pocus, and using an "eye" to scare them away. I listened, interested in the culture and history of the Gullah, even if I didn't believe in their superstitions.

"Roger gave me one of those 'evil eye' beads on my first trip," I interjected.

"Well, where is it?" Jack wanted to know.

"I have no idea," I confessed. "I thought he was just trying to spook me."

"She doesn't believe in ghosts," Donny pointed out. They both shook their heads disapprovingly.

The golf cart was fully charged when we pulled away from Jack's house, but I no longer trusted the vehicle. Convinced it was a faulty battery, I traded out golf carts when we returned to Haig Point. Donny went straight to his computer to download photos. I pulled off my boots and tried to relax. A sharp rap on my door interrupted the peace. It was Donny, pale and agitated.

"Take a look at the pictures I took today," he said as he led me down the hall.

I sat at his computer and flipped through hundreds of photographs. *Early morning mist rising over the tabby ruins at Haig Point... copperhead hiding in the grass... slave cemetery... Bloody Point... baloney sandwich... tomato juice dripping down my chin... giant deer tick... me poking my head into the Oyster House... ramshackle stairs.*

"Now, look what happens when I stitch the shots together that I took upstairs," he said. He pushed a button, and I saw what I had missed at the Oyster House. The image showed an eerily beautiful space, abandoned to time and the elements. But the most compelling aspect of the picture was the middle of the room, smeared, as though the lens was completely out of focus.

"That fuzzy part," he said, "was when I photographed the wall that made the *noise*." The last word materialized in a frantic whisper.

"That's just coincidence," I argued.

"Ok," he said. "Then let's look at a second round of photos going back the other direction." I watched. The strange glow again obscured the center of the photo.

"Convinced?" Donny asked.

"No," I said.

We ate dinner at Marshside Mamma's. The power level on the new golf cart had sunk to "E" right as we passed the turnoff for the Oyster House on the way to restaurant, so we plugged it in while we waited on our food. News of our haint problem had spread quickly and many of the locals began sharing their own tales of supernatural experiences on the island. Several had phantom images appear in photographs. Many had weird feelings or experiences they could not explain.

"I see ghosts," Clarence said matter-of-factly.

He was one of the few Gullah left on the island. He worked a variety of jobs around the island, and we often saw him, although he always ignored us. I chalked that up to the fact we were just a couple of *Comeyas*. Perhaps it was our brush with a haint that made Clarence friendly that night. Maybe he simply felt like talking. His story was so straight forward I know he believed what he told us, and it was enough to make me second guess my doubts.

"When do you see ghosts?" I asked.

"Every night. And some mornings, too. I see the children."

"What children?"

"I see the children that lived in my house and died. They run around my bed. Sometime they laugh. Sometimes they want to play games."

"You actually see them?" I asked.

"A little girl and a little boy. The girl has her hair all done up in braids. I just stay put in my bed until they go away."

That was all Clarence would say on the subject. When later I asked for more details, he ignored me with such purpose I knew that had been the one and only story he would ever share with me.

Donny and I barely made it back to Haig Point that night, the needle showing the golf cart's power level jumping up and down like decibel gage on a disco speaker. But the Mammaritas we had imbibed did wonders to ease our anxiety, and I would later blame what happened on tequila.

As I floated to sleep, I had the sensation I could not breathe. I remember telling myself to wake up, and I was quite aware I was having a strange dream in a strange bed on a strange island. But I could never quite pull myself into wakefulness, and the sense of suffocating lasted until 9 a.m. when Donny rapped on my door.

He came bearing coffee, which we enjoyed on the piazza. He seemed well rested – even his coloring was normal – but that all changed as I told him about my dream.

"Oh, God, Susan," he said, taking on the pallor of a bleached oyster shell. "You might have picked up a *hag!*"

I wanted to plead a more reasonable explanation, but we did not have time to argue about ghosts. Shaking my head, I closed the door and left Donny to contemplate Gullah spirits. I needed to focus on the project. An archaeologist was scheduled to arrive on the 10:30 ferry – a professional to help us identify, photograph, and catalog a ten-thousand-year spectrum of Native American pottery – and I didn't want to welcome him in pajamas.

Donny and I watched as the residents and guests filed off the ferry. All but one was over the age of sixty and wearing golf attire. On some unconscious level I suppose I expected our archaeologist to look like Indiana Jones. If not Harrison Ford, then maybe the older Dr. Jones, played by Sean Connery. When the last passenger disembarked, we found ourselves staring at a boyish character wearing jeans and a backpack.

"That must be Alex," I said in surprise.

"He can't be our archaeologist," Donny protested. "That kid isn't old enough to drive a golf cart."

In fact, Alex was old enough to have earned a Master's Degree in Archaeology, and he was kind enough to volunteer his Saturday to help us sort and identify pre-Columbian pottery. I thought the nicest way to repay his favor was to give him a tour of the island. Donny thought the best course of action was to scare him to pieces with ghost stories.

I could tell Alex was in my camp, meaning he was politely listening to Donny's warnings of hags and haints, but he didn't really believe in them. He was certainly interested in the stories, but in a detached anthropological way, as a means to fill in the gaps left by dust and bone.

We treated him to the best lunch on the island, Craig's fried baloney sandwich, and sat outside the marina watching the tide roll in. I told him all I knew of the history of Daufuskie, its formation during the last ice age, the climate and soil makeup, the Native American sites, the profitable indigo and cotton plantations, and the famous oyster industry. Donny would interject with details of our golf cart running dead, unexplained noises, phantom photos, and a ghost nearly killing me in my four-poster bed at The Mansion.

Alex and I humored Donny, but we were both eager to put talk of ghosts aside and head to far end of the island to meet a friend who had one of the largest collections of Native American pottery sherds on Daufuskie. As we drove off with another new, fully-charged golf cart, needle showing "F," an October storm blew onto the island. The rain flew at us sideways, and we had to unroll the plastic sheeting on our cart in a feeble attempt to keep dry.

To get to the pottery, we had to pass by the road to the oyster house. By the time we hit the turn off, we were thoroughly soaked, but not so distracted that we missed seeing the needle of the battery gage swing from "F" to "E."

"See that!" Donny screamed at us with vindication. "That is a haint."

We made it to our destination, heart skipping with every random swing in the power level. After Donny's fantastic stories of haints and hags, Alex was amazed that my reports about the pottery were true. Buckets, barrels, and boxes overflowed with museum-quality specimens.

Two hours of looking through a remarkable collection of pottery helped bolster our mood. But we couldn't stay there forever, and the storm was still wailing when we said our goodbyes, thanking our host for letting us look through her collection and for allowing us to plug in and recharge our temperamental golf cart.

Our threesome remained silent as we rolled down the dirt road toward the turn off. We watched the needle. My blood turned as cold as my rain-soaked toes when, as we passed the road leading to the Oyster House, the hand jumped twice and then settled back at "E." Donny shouted out against the rain, and poor Alex choked back a sob.

For me, the thought of a ghost was terrifying, but it was not as unsettling as the prospect of being stranded in hurricane-type conditions on a road in the middle of nowhere. It was doubtful any sane person would be riding around in such a miserable storm to offer rescue. Running out of juice meant we would slush back on foot several miles, and Alex would certainly miss his ferry.

By some miracle, or whim of our meddlesome haint, the golf cart continued forward at the maddening pace of *barely moving.* For more than an hour we three, sad, sorry, soggy adventurers prayed, laughed, crossed our fingers, and cried as we inched forward toward the ferry. We rolled through the gates at a quarter after four and staggered to the dock at 4:28 p.m., just as the captain was about to pull the gangway.

"Thanks, Alex," I said. "You really helped with the project." We had been through so much together in those cold, wet hours. In place of the child-like innocence he had projected on arrival, I saw a somber, beaten-down expression. He almost looked his age.

"Bye, man," Donny said. I could tell he, too, was sad to see our sidekick go, but I would never have guessed what he said next. "I just hope the haint doesn't follow you back home."

As Alex jumped onto the ferry I saw him visibly shudder, and I do not believe it was from cold.

"Why did you do that?" I scolded Donny.

"Because…" Donny said flatly. "If things start happening to that boy, he needs to know why."

I don't know if the haint followed Alex across the river, or if she just tired of the game and left us all, but from that moment forward Donny and I had no more problems with golf carts.

Over the next year, the Daufuskie Island Historical Society renovated the dilapidated Oyster House to preserve what was left of the structure, making it a sanctioned stop on the official history tour. Once again, Donny and I shuttled across Daufuskie by golf cart. We wanted to see it for ourselves.

"Goodness!" I said as we rolled up to the door and walked across newly-manicured grounds.

We stared at the wall where we picked up the haint. Instead of splinters and wavy wooden planks, we saw new siding and a fresh coat of paint. It was just too much. We both burst into fits of laughter.

"What the heck do you think happened to the guy who tackled those renovations?" Donny asked when he could finally string words together. "I mean… all *we* did was take a few *pictures*!"

"I bet he's still out there somewhere," I answered. "Stranded on a golf cart."

A Bushel and a Peck

Kathryn Etters Lovatt

Before real summer sets in, something very much like a peach comes to market. Leathery skin wraps around leathery innards, the flesh of the fruit clings whole-heartedly to its pit.

These early pickings are scrawny, tragically devoid of scent, and perfectly irresistible. My father used to scorn them. "Bah," he'd proclaim, "a May peach," although the next month would be well upon us.

We ate them anyway, him complaining and me resigned. A May peach, or a June one for that matter, is better than no peach at all.

Later, in the height of full harvest, we'd stand side-by-side and devour dead-ripe Redhavens over the huge double sink of my parents' kitchen. There, in those months, in those moments of immeasurable abundance, the true and imagined stories of my young life still play out. In the background, tractors drone like a soundtrack. Outside, it's dripping hot.

In the baby-booming deep South of the Fifties, summers felt as if the blazing fist of Vulcan, Roman god of fire, punched through the sky and landed a blow in the middle of South Carolina. Temperatures rose to the danger zone as school let out for the year. The thermometer refused to back down until after Labor Day, the longstanding signal for classes to start again.

The stinging heat drove up vines, bolted stalks, and would, in due time, turn tomatoes brilliant red. Garden patches tendered okra, peppers, melons, corn, far too many squash, and every kind of bean ever cultivated.

Although lone air-conditioners teeter-tottered in windows of privilege, most everyone took shelter on porches or under shade trees. Church fans and fly swatters were held in high regard. Even early mornings swarmed with pesky things that stung or bit or, scarier still, might strike.

My big brother happily ran amok in the fields and swamps, but I was too young to go my own way. A few weeks into summer vacation, a muggy boredom began settling over me early in the afternoon when not even our dogs showed interest in play. They dug holes and hunkered down in the cool dirty-dirt below a beach-like layer of white sand. A sharp twig to the homes of doodlebugs failed to persuade a one to surface. And ants had laid claim to the climbable mimosa.

My mother carried the daily weight of me looking for something to do as long as she could. That took us roughly through lunch.

"All right," she'd say as she put away the final plate.

Momma put me in the car and drove nearly fifteen miles to her mother's. Grandma did not suffer whiners.

We entered by a side door straight into the kitchen, a room we hardly ever left while inside. Rather than the aroma of baking cookies, the savory smell of streak-of-lean, cousin-once-removed to poor fatback, filled my grandmother's house. This esteemed all-purpose seasoning of old southern cooks could have been detected even if nothing bubbled on the stove eye or roasted in the oven—although I recall no such occasion.

If Grandma wasn't baking, she was canning; she blanched, pickled, or jellied whatever ripened. She gloried in what looked like drudgery, particularly for a woman her size, a powerhouse of a redhead who came from days when mills worked children of twelve, she among them. Perhaps that early hard labor set in motion the belief that no one, on any account, should sit idle.

Oblivious to the heat rising in vapors from her stove, she would, for our sakes, fling open the back and front doors and send me to flip the switch to her attic fan. A cyclone ensued.

Any piece of loose paper lifted, briefly floated, then scattered. Selma, the wide-bottomed calico cat, twitched her tail at whatever happened to fly by.

That stiff wind carried no power to cool by day, only the draw of the soft night air could do that, but pointing out the fan's failings might be interpreted as a complaint. If griping was a symptom of sloth, work was its tonic, and Grandma never fell short of chores even a little girl might do: drying silverware, filling a wheelbarrow with pinecones, dusting. The one task I never minded started out with the lowly bean.

A man with a truckload of vegetables pulled regularly into the road by my grandmother's house. He came early mornings, first to her—or so he said, and so she believed—to let her take the pick of his produce.

On those days, my mother and I would arrive and find a pitcher of grape Kool-Aid, iced and waiting. Grandma went straight to her draped dining room, and out she would come with a split-wood basket, tall and conical, brimming beyond its bushel walls with something so fresh, bugs thrived on the outside and gorged themselves with what lay within.

Grandma's very favorite something was beans, better still if they were butterbeans, and best of all, speckled butterbeans. Not simply colored, mind you.

No matter what the sciences assert, there is indeed a difference. Raw speckled beans glisten like semi-precious stones. They brandish the purples of amethyst, from pale lavender to veins shocked with port wine. They shine like opals, translucent gems traced with fire. From experience, I know this to be true, and I know that before their full array can be properly admired, a veritable heap of them must be shelled.

Our shelling took place on the front porch. My mother and I always sat on the green glider, an enamel pan between us. My grandmother, in one of two matching rockers, always expected her younger daughter any minute.

My aunt—she of weak wrist and a Friday standing appointment with Audrey, queen bee of hair-dos and manicures in our small realm—usually showed up. We were begrudgingly glad to see her.

Aunt Mae pulled her chair from our circle, outside the breeze of the Emerson table fan, black and heavy as cast iron. Powered by a frazzled tail of a cord, the blades turned like dervishes, high being the one and only speed, and the force certainly would have mussed my aunt's French twist.

Her distance from the three of us also separated Mae from the tower of beans and the communal aluminum catch-all for spent shells. She spent most of her energy going up and down to dispose of an empty pod or two and adding her meager garner to Grandma's pool of beans. Never mind. We were together, a fact as important to our rhythm as the task before us.

A butterbean shell is like an oyster. The sides hold together in a clamp and the knife that opens the coupling is your thumbnail. This single gesture should split the shell wide open and the beans spill out with the slightest nudge. Simple enough.

But the juices and the repeated motion offend the tender quick beneath the nail and rub the surrounding skin raw. And yet, we gathered eagerly. The others' mouths might have watered at the prospect of speckled beans with a side of biscuit, but I wasn't there for the beans. I was there for the talk.

This was our campfire, a solitary time and place to tell tales. Grandma did most of the telling. Sometimes she began with healers and dreamers of dreams, stories from the Bible, but in short order she fell back into the unfathomable mire of horror. Edgar Allen Poe had nothing on her. Time and again, she scared me speechless with body parts in cellars, whispers in the night, a dead woman tapping at the window.

I can only suppose my mother allowed me to hear about people being buried alive because she wanted to hear about people being buried alive. In any case, these anecdotes could be depended upon to quicken the pace of our shelling.

Grandma's best story, a ghost story she vowed to be true, was told in first person. It took place, naturally, one dark and stormy night.

A crack of lightning and a pounding on the door roused her. She didn't nudge my grandfather awake—she wasn't that kind of a woman—but got up out of bed and went to the door. There, drenching wet, stood Uncle Hazard, kin from my grandfather's side, kin who lived an entire state away. He shook himself off as she unlatched the screen.

"What in the world are you doing here?" my grandmother asked as she ushered him in.

He'd paid a visit to his son in Columbia he told her and thought he would stop by and say hello.

"Let me go tell Tyrie," she said, referring to my grandfather, Tyra.

But by the time Granddaddy pulled on his pants, threw on a shirt and got to the living room, no one was there.

"He was standing in this very spot." Grandmother pointed to a damp ring by the door. "What on earth made him go?"

My grandparents decided to telephone in the morning. Calling long distance was not an everyday event. Or someone called them. Or maybe it was one way one time, and another the next.

I didn't care. Still don't, because to this day, the story gives me a satisfying chill. Of course, Uncle Hazard had died in his bed that same night.

This was not a story my grandmother told every time we shelled beans, but it was definitely a bean story, and one she could almost always be persuaded to tell if they were speckled.

To everyone's surprise, my grandmother *was* mere flesh and blood. She left this world without coming to anybody's door.

From the memory of watching my grandmother, my mother cooked the foods of her mother's life and of her own. She searched each summer for beans.

One year, she heard about a shelling machine, and she wanted to take a look. I drove her thirty miles down roads only my father, a former rural mail carrier, and the family who lived at the dusty end must have been able to find with ease.

A man brought out a big plastic bag. Mother held the bag up, inspected the mangled contents inside, and handed the bag back. We left without a single bean. Technology had a ways to go before it could mechanically shell and leave the beans intact.

A few years later, a place named Lee's Peas and Beans opened up. Theirs were shelled, but whole and firm. They had some speckled ones, or maybe they were only colored. We bought a bushel. The woman who sold them to us turned to me.

"Do you blanch your beans?" she asked.

I looked at Mother. She nodded.

"We do," I said.

The woman, deferring again to my mother's age and careful perhaps not to question experience, delivered her advice to me instead.

"If you take them home and wash the field dust off real good and just put them in a bag and cover them with water, I think you'll be satisfied."

My mother had to speak up then. "Don't blanch them?"

"No ma'am."

"Hrumph," my mother said in the car. "I'll try one quart."

She pulled her test bag of beans from the freezer not long after and cooked them as usual. They tasted like they came fresh from the garden. She shook her head.

"I'll be," was all she had to say.

After that, we looked for Lee's truck or drove to the farm, but once or twice a season, Momma would find a mess of beans in the store or by the road and buy them both for old time's sake and because a bean out of the shell and into the pot is like a trout from the brook to the pan.

We would sit at the table, my mother, father, and me, and later my daughter Brie would take a chair. Sometimes, oh, nearly every time, I would say, "Remember that awful story Grandma told about Uncle Hazard?"

But Momma would act like she couldn't quite, so I would have to tell every detail and add a few of my own.

As we sat there popping open shells and tossing the contents into the bowl my mother inherited, I realized the beans were never as purple as in my imagination. Still, they made a sweet little sound as they hit the enamel. *Plink, plink-plonk,* they sang, every bean adding to the pile, every note adding to the tune.

*First Published in *What I Wish I Could Tell You,* Waxing Crescent Press, December, 2016.

Summer in the Sandhills

Sherry Fasano

The early morning sun shone through the jalousie window and highlighted the blue floral pattern on the porcelain tea set. I stood on tiptoes in front of the kitchen buffet and counted one- two- three- four- five- six- seven- eight- nine- ten miniature pieces, neatly packaged in a cellophane lidded box. I had never seen anything more beautiful.

The smell of perking coffee filled Aunt Celia's kitchen. As soon as my three younger cousins woke, her attention would be divided between them. But for now, she placed a plate of corned beef hash and hot buttered biscuits dripping with cane syrup on the table and smiled.

I smiled back.

I loved summer days spent at Aunt Celia's in the Sandhills of South Carolina. The woods behind Grandaddy's pasture kept my cousins and me busy until Mama's workday downtown was over. We created sand villages for our miniature cars and trucks, arranged nurseries for our dolls out of fragrant pine straw, and cooked for each other in pretend kitchens, undisturbed until we were called in for lunch.

Our kitchens in the woods were outfitted with castoff utensils from Grandmama's and Aunt Celia's kitchens. Sometimes we snuck Saltine crackers back there, and I coaxed my younger cousins to season them from cracked salt and pepper shakers filled with powdery grey dirt.

We learned how to fill a rusty cake pan with a mixture of loamy sand and water from the creek and turn out perfectly formed mud cakes. White sand sprinkled over the top and wild flowers decorated these elaborate cakes. By summer's end and with our skills perfected, we could cut the mud cakes and serve our dolls thin slices on tiny plates.

Aunt Celia kept a metal washtub filled with water by the back door, so we could wash our dirty bare feet before coming inside for a lunch of Kool-Aide and a bologna sandwich. After that, she expected us to go back outside and entertain ourselves for the rest of the afternoon.

Some afternoons we climbed the Hackberry trees at the edge of the pasture and called out to Grandaddy's cows. Curious, they slowly moved toward us, but stopped a safe distance away. The bravest one of them, Mary-Belle, often walked forward, stretched her neck, and stared at us with big brown eyes. If we walked over to the fence slowly and spoke quietly, she allowed us to reach through the fence and pat her muzzle. But if we talked loudly or yelled, she turned away, and with the bell around her neck clang-clanging, led the others back to the other side of the pasture where they grazed on sweet green grass.

At least once we found trouble while playing on our own. One hot afternoon, Grandaddy's septic tank overflowed in the field between his house and Aunt Celia's. I convinced my cousins to 'swim' in the muddy pool, and we stripped down to our underwear and splashed each other until Aunt Celia spotted us. We knew we were in trouble when she ran toward us, shouting and waving her arms.

She herded us home with a thin switch from the spiraea bush by the fence and dunked us, one by one, in the old metal washtub full of cold, soapy water. While she scrubbed us clean, she looked toward heaven and prayed aloud, "Lord, please protect these children from the Typhoid Fever. And if you have time, Lord, could you help them behave like good little children should?"

Later, on particularly trying days, she again looked toward heaven and declared, "At least He heard one of my prayers."

Every Thursday morning, we all squeezed into Grandmama's big Ford and drove to town. At Woolworth's dime store, Grandmama doled out a quarter to each of us to spend while she and Aunt Celia searched for hair-pins and cold cream. My cousins and I perused the toy aisle and fingered the cheap plastic toys until we all decided on the same thing. Most often, we chose miniature troll dolls with long rainbow colored hair, or small metal cars and trucks to add to our sand village.

Our next stop was the Winn-Dixie. After we bought groceries and loaded the trunk of the car with heavy brown paper bags, Aunt Celia drove us to Curly's hot dog stand. Grandmama insisted we take the hot dogs home to eat because it was rumored Curly served B-E-E-R.

The smell of chili and onions coming from that bag of hot dogs filled the car, making our stomachs growl. And by the time we arrived home and unloaded all the groceries, the hotdogs were just lukewarm, but we never complained. We gulped them down along with the 'Thursday only' Co-Colas we were allowed each week.

Twice a month, the cousins and I stayed with Grandmama while Aunt Celia shopped alone. Since my uncle served in the Air Force, she enjoyed Commissary privileges and spent the better part of those days buying groceries.

Before she left, Aunt Celia arranged her hair in a pouffy French Twist and dressed in a skirt and blouse and Ked's. Then, she kissed each one of us on the cheek and promised to bring us a surprise.

Usually, the surprise was a fifteen cents box of Cracker Jacks. As soon as she gave them to us, we excitedly crunched our way through the sticky caramel corn and peanuts and searched for the small toy prize hidden in the bottom of the box. We never ceased hoping the next box held something really valuable, something like a genuine rhinestone ring or a Cinderella watch.

On Aunt Celia's grocery days, Grandmama restricted us to her backyard because she worried a bit more than Aunt Celia. Thunderstorms especially scared her. Whenever the sky darkened with storm clouds, she immediately called us inside and pointed to the bedroom where we piled onto the tall bed.

She unplugged everything electric, and then sternly cautioned us, "Alright children, let's be real quiet now, it's a certainty lightening follows loud noises."

One of us always made a funny face, and the rest fell into giggles. With her finger to her lips, she shushed, "I don't want to hear one more peep."

And, of course, somebody "peeped."

More giggles. But by the end of the storm, we were sprawled across the chenille bedspread sleeping soundly. We woke with the bedspread design imprinted on our cheeks and the window fan pulling a rain freshened breeze through the window screens.

A special treat were the afternoons Grandaddy called from the pasture, "Blackberry pickin' time!"

We each grabbed the closest container we could find, climbed the fence, and followed him like he was the Pied Piper, picking his way through the briars and pointing out the juiciest berries.

Grandmama had the oven heated by the time we returned. We sat out on the back porch steps and rubbed spit on our red-bug bites until she served us bowls of hot, buttery crusted cobbler.

Once in a while, Aunt Celia announced a watermelon cutting. This was an even bigger treat. It meant Grandaddy had a watermelon on ice and, *if we behaved* she stressed, later that afternoon we'd be summoned to Grandmama's backyard to enjoy the cold melon. We behaved. And when Grandaddy called, we raced next door.

We clamored around the picnic table while he cut the watermelon. When the melon thwacked open and he handed each of us a dripping slice, we dove in, face first, spitting seeds right onto the patio. Then at each other.

After we ate our fill and he threw all the gnawed-white rinds over into the chicken pen, Grandaddy squirted the sticky off of us and the patio with the garden hose, and we stretched out in the warm grass to dry.

Sometimes while we lay in the grass, Grandaddy told outrageous stories. But most of the time he simply sang, "The one who loves me best, is bound to kiss me first...the one who loves me best will kiss me first."

In our rush to kiss him, somebody usually got elbowed and cried. But Grandaddy charmed the hurt away by scratching his head and promising, "Look here, young'uns, tell you what. I'll give the first one of you to find a louse in my hair a whole green dollar bill. Yep, there's likely one in there, you just gotta look real close to find it."

We each one fingered his thick brown hair carefully, but never one time found any sort of creature. He was snoring by the time we grew bored.

Though happy to see Mama when she drove into Aunt Celia's driveway in the late afternoons, I often wished I could stay just a little longer. Aunt Celia was busy cooking supper this time of the day because Uncle Frank was due home. And Uncle Frank liked to eat. The smells from her kitchen made my stomach growl. Smells of fried chicken, whipped potatoes, green beans from her garden, and freshly baked cornbread.

More importantly though, were the sounds. Aunt Celia sang while she cooked. Her clear voice drifted out of the window screens and into the woods where we played,

"There is a name I love to hear,

I love to sing its worth;

It sounds like music in my ear,

The sweetest name on earth.

Oh how I love Jesus,

Oh how I love Jesus,

Oh how I love Jesus,

Because He first loved me!"

That same summer day when I first spied the tea set, I wasn't ready to leave when Mama came to collect me. I cried.

The day had been full of adventure. My youngest cousin had spotted a threaded needle in the bathroom and snuck it back to the creek where an abundance of tadpoles had recently grown into baby frogs. She commenced stringing a squirming baby frog necklace.

When her sister ran home and tattled, Aunt Celia marched to the creek, hands on hips, and insisted she unstring them. Then, filled with belated compassion, we created a creek side hospital with rows of beds fashioned from pecan shells.

Because the threaded needle was fine gauged, though, the baby frogs seemed unfazed, and we had a hard time keeping them in their beds. So my cousins really needed my help and pleaded with Mama, "Aunt Maxine, just a little bit longer, plee-ease Aunt Maxine?"

But Mama shook her head no and said we needed to hurry on home.

Aunt Celia smiled and motioned for Mama to wait, and then she winked at me, "Hold on a minute, sweet pea. I almost forgot your surprise from the Commissary."

When she returned from the kitchen, I expected a box of Cracker Jacks. But a few minutes later I walked out the door, smiling and clutching the box with the blue and white tea set to my chest with one hand and holding Mama's hand with the other. In my mind, I was already planning a tea party for the baby frogs the next morning.

The Legend of a Good Man

L. Thomas-Cook

On August 18, 1913, Sheriff William James White of Spartanburg, South Carolina, and a single deputy, faced an angry, volatile mob of over 1,000 people who gathered ready to take the law into their own hands. The sheriff would not tolerate it. He stood tall and self-assured as he stared into the eyes of so many he knew well.

The crowd that rallied outside the jailhouse showed no remorse and glared back with enraged faces, shirt sleeves rolled up, and demanded their version of justice.

Sheriff White, his rifle at ease pointed down by his side, put up his hand to silence the shouts. "Gentlemen," he said, "I hate to do it, but so help me God I'm going to kill the first man that enters that gate."

The late summer air hung thick with heat brought on, not just from the humidity common for the south, but also from raw, self-righteous anger. What had sparked such vicious reactions in this growing and prosperous city? An African-American man, accused of sexually assaulting a young, white woman, a resident of the small community, was being held for trial. The man accused was William Fair.

Gossip of what had occurred spread like mosquitoes on a rainy night. Once the white citizens of Spartanburg heard that one of their own had been violated, they took guns, axes, bats, and canes straight to the jail house.

"Bring the negro out here," Jed Baker shouted. The crowd of fifty stood belligerent behind him and demanded the same. Before long, fifty grew into a hundred. Then into a thousand.

"Can't do that, Jed. You know I can't," Sheriff White said. "The law's the law. He's accused, but he gets a trial to decide the truth. Same for everyone."

"He ain't like everyone," Pete Simms shouted. "He ain't nothing like me."

"Or me," other voices joined in.

"We want justice," the crowd chanted.

"We're going to get him, Sheriff, one way or the other," a voice Sheriff White thought he recognized threatened from within the mob. He heard others shout, too. Some voices were familiar, but their faces were hidden from sight. It didn't matter. He was well aware of their prejudice.

During the 19th century, Spartanburg was like many other towns and cities throughout the south. The Ku Klux Klan was embedded in the culture even though by the earlier nineteen-hundreds the number of black business owners, police, and firefighters, as well as those who held city council seats, had significantly grown.

Even so, racial violence continued to oppress and thrive. Police records contain numerous reports of hostile mobs with narrow minds taking justice into their own hands. Actions of malice and ignorance without care for true vindication of the victim were as common as alligators in the southern marsh.

Less than a week before Fair's arrest, a black man accused of a similar crime in a county not far from Spartanburg was lynched. Pulled from his jail cell by a large, irate mob and dragged to the railroad tracks, the mob then tossed a rope over the old willow tree. The man hanged while his pleas of innocence were ignored. He never received a trial. He never had a chance to defend himself in a court of law.

"Settle down," the sheriff said to the restless mass. "We're better than this. Jed? Sam? Jack? Come on. You know me. This is not how to get things done."

"It's how they got it done in Laurens County," Jack said.

The crowd cheered and raised their weapons in the air.

"You thought you could keep the whole arrest quiet," Jed hollered. "Well you haven't fooled nobody, Sheriff. We demand his black neck in a noose. No colored folks come here and get away with anything. Not in our city."

"What should we do?" the deputy by White's side said. The sheriff sensed his shaking.

"We let them come to their senses." Sheriff White put up one hand to speak to the crowd. "Just calm down. The suspect has a right to a trial—"

"You mean the black rapist," someone yelled. The crowd cheered again.

"I mean the man accused," the sheriff answered, his voice loud and strong. "Once his court date is scheduled and he gets his fair say in court, we'll proceed according to law."

Sheriff White glanced with calm and confident resolve into as many eyes as he could. A few lowered their heads and shifted back and forth, but not Jed Baker. He glared dark eyes straight at the sheriff. Like two stubborn bulls, he and the sheriff stared at one another. The only thing missing was smoke coming out of their noses and feet stomping the ground.

"This isn't about either one of us, Jed," the sheriff said. "This is about the law and a man's right." He broke eye contact with Jed and spoke to the crowd. "I'm not saying he isn't guilty or that he is. I'm saying as good men, and all of you are, that we give him a fair trial and listen to the evidence. Let a jury decide. That's how it's done. How good men do it.

Now go on home. Your wives probably have supper ready. There's no more to be done here today."

Jed Baker scoffed, the corner of his lip curled up. He backed away slowly. "Okay, sheriff. Whatever you say." He turned to the crowd. "Let's go boys."

Pete frowned at him. "But, Jed, you said we'd...."

"Never you mind that." Jed glanced over his shoulder at the sheriff. "Just do what I tell ya."

The crowd marched down the street behind Jed and Pete. They spoke in harsh, low tones, and kicked up dust as they wandered away.

Sheriff White kept an eye on the group as they dispersed. He looked at his deputy, noticed the sweat across the younger man's forehead, and handed him a handkerchief. "It's okay," he said and patted the deputy on the arm. "Let's get inside."

"Sheriff? I don't think Jed plans to let this go." The deputy wiped his brow. "It's not like him. He's as pig headed as they come. I saw him come face to face with a cotton mouth snake once. The snake backed down. Jed didn't. He chased it into the woods and didn't come back out until he had it cut in half dangling from his knife."

"I know," the sheriff said. "Let's get inside. Load the rifles. I'll try reaching the mayor again."

Less than an hour of strained quiet passed, just enough time to either relax or get ready. Sheriff White knew better than to relax. At 5:00 p.m. a dynamite blast rang out. The exterior jailhouse wall crumbled. The recharged mob of 1,000 stormed the jail. As the dust and flying cinderblock settled, Sheriff White grabbed his rifle and stood between the mob and the jail.

"I won't warn you again," he shouted. "So help me, I will shoot." He raised the rifle and pointed it upward. Jed and three men took a step forward. Sheriff White fired a warning shot into the air. The mob backed away.

With the crowd on the street outside in a huddle like a football team planning the next offense, Sheriff White told his deputy to watch the group. He rushed back inside to his phone and called the Spartanburg mayor and Governor Coleman Blease for help to disperse the crowd. Both men refused.

"Damn it." Sheriff White slammed his fist on the desk.

"Sheriff?" the deputy yelled, "They're coming back."

The sheriff ran to the outer room and through the ten-foot hole from the blast, watched as Jed Baker and fourteen other men stormed toward them.

The sheriff and deputy turned and hurried to the back room where they slammed shut the gate that led to the jail cells and locked it. As the sheriff turned around again, Jed Baker and the others charged through the gaping hole with a battering ram, rushed to the back, and attempted to smash down the gate.

"We told you, sheriff," Jed hollered, "We want justice." They slammed into the gate again. Pieces of the wooden battering ram splintered. Chunks flew into the air.

"And I told you," the sheriff lifted his gun, "justice is what we all want but not like this."

The men, seven on each side of the large wooden beam, rushed the gate once more. The steel shook.

Sheriff White fired several shots into the air. Plaster rained down all around them. The men charged the gate, again. Sheriff White aimed his gun at Jed.

Jed put up his hands. "Get back," he shouted to the others. They backed out onto the street. From behind them a second group attempted to charge forward.

Sheriff White and the deputy rushed outside to the front steps of the jailhouse. They fired shots into the crowd. The mob stopped and fired back.

With no cover from the crowd, the sheriff shouted to his deputy, "Get inside." He and the deputy retreated behind what remained of the bombed-out wall. Hundreds of pistol shots were fired from both sides. Bullets ricocheted off the stone, others whizzed by the sheriff's head.

Concerned for his young deputy, Sheriff White shouted to him to get back further. The sheriff ducked behind the wall. He placed himself between the crazed mob and his deputy, the shots he returned to the crowd were intended to warn or to wound, not to kill.

"This has gotten out of hand, Jed," the sheriff shouted as he reloaded his weapon. "Stop before someone gets killed."

"Can't do that, sheriff." Jed hid along the corner wall of the general store directly across from the jailhouse. "Give us the negro, and we'll leave."

"My job is to protect all the citizens of this county." The sheriff saw Jed's shirt tail flap in the breeze. "That means everybody not just the few." He aimed his gun with a clear shot, but chose to shoot the ground at Jim's feet.

"Come on, sheriff, you're a better shot than that." Jed fired. More bullet blasts chipped away at the compromised wall – the only means of cover for the sheriff and the deputy.

Sheriff White glanced over at his deputy and sighed. He stood, exposed for a moment, and shot. Jed's right leg went out from under him, blood oozed from his calf.

The newspapers later reported that no one knew how long the two men stood alone against the crowd. For the sheriff and his deputy it seemed an eternity. The city police department finally arrived, but only after Jed Baker and two other men in the crowd were injured. The mob broke up, and Will Fair, trembling in his cell under his cot, was transported to a jail in Columbia to await trial.

Over a century later, the scene and all it meant is still remembered. "My great-great uncle was a hell of a man," Sheriff White's nephew, Michael Smith, was reported to say. "I grew up listening to this story. It's been a legend passed down from generation to generation."

It would be a month until the trial began. It's a sure bet that during that time Sheriff White went to Jed Baker and the others to warn them not to attempt any more violence toward him, his deputy, or any black members of the community.

"There better be no more of this nonsense," the sheriff may have said to those responsible for the ambush. "No burning buildings. No one touched or harmed in any way. Because it doesn't matter if any of you hide under sheets, the eyes betray the soul."

"I've always heard how proud the family was of him," Michael Smith said. "I just never stopped to think about or appreciate what he faced in that city every day."

On September 20, 1913, a special session of the court was convened in Spartanburg County. On this day, everyone would hear what actually happened.

On the day of the incident, Will Fair began his day as he normally did, with his seven-mile walk from the small town of Glendale to the Spartanburg train station. Fair passed several people, but paid them no mind.

According to the victim, a young woman whose name was withheld from the newspapers, the accused followed her into her home, hitting her over the head and raping her. She reported it, and Fair was quickly arrested.

Will Fair was a resident in the county with a population of about 85,000 people, of which 32 percent were black. Spartanburg, with its slogan, 'City of Success,' was growing but even so, like many southern areas, it had its share of growing pains.

But despite the victim's testimony that she put up a fight, a police officer called to the scene, who, after getting Will Fair's name and locating him at the train station within minutes of the complaint, reported that there were no rips or stains of any kind to Fair's clothing. Fair's clothes also did not match what the victim described her attacker wearing.

The officer claimed there would have been no time for the defendant to change prior to the arrest. Will Fair lived miles away from the city and appeared to be quietly waiting for the train. Another officer called to the stand testified that the victim identified a different man as the assailant before accusing Fair, but changed her mind later.

Additional witnesses testified that they saw Fair and the woman on the same path headed down the street, but no one ever saw Fair go into the woman's house. A doctor, known to many in the city, took the stand and when asked if he examined the victim, he attested he had.

"What was the result of that examination, doctor?" Fair's attorney asked.

"I found no bruises or other signs of physical trauma from the assault," the doctor said.

A gasp and whispered murmurs filled the court room. Judge George Gage banged his mallet and ordered the spectators to be quiet.

"We rest our case," attorneys from both sides said. Will Fair's lawyer quietly sat next to his somber client.

Judge Gage handed the case to the jury followed by instructions to the 12 all white jurors. He looked each one in the eye and said, "I cannot impress upon you the importance of this case. Your decision, fair and impartial, will become a part of this city, this county, this country for all time."

Later Gage was reported to say, "A case like this not only tries the prisoner at the bar, but it even tries the very integrity of our institutions."

As the jury shuffled out of the court, Fair remained seated. His hands shook and his eyes, which never looked anywhere except straight ahead, held worry. He sighed heavily and finally stood, shook his attorney's hand and gave a nod toward Sheriff White.

Hours passed. The jury foreman came back to the judge several times stating the jury was deadlocked. "We need a mistrial, Judge," he said. "We have six jurors who want to find Fair not guilty and six others that agree, but no one wants to put it on record. They want another jury to pass the decision."

The judge refused the request each time the foreman returned to his chambers. "A wave of public opinion in times of excitement is sometimes the most uncertain thing in the world," Judge Gage said and rested his hand on a thick book of law and statues. "The only certain thing is the knowledge which points to the truth and which never errs. If you follow it, you are in the sure path, and if you leave it, you are in quagmires all the way."

Just after noon on September 20, 1913, the jury reached a decision. Spectators from around the county jammed themselves into every square inch of the courtroom.

Judge Gage ordered everyone in the room to remain quiet. "As the verdict is read I expect everyone in here to refrain from any outburst. I want absolute quiet as the decision is given and after. Deputies are here to escort anyone, and I mean anyone, who decides to ignore this court."

His face stoic, he looked at Sheriff White who returned a reassuring nod.

Sheriff White, arms crossed, stood by the closed courtroom door in the back. He scanned the room. Jed Baker, his right leg wrapped in a bandage and his left arm still in a sling from the gunshot wounds, sat in the middle left row of the section reserved for whites. Next to him sat the three other men who had tried to batter the jail house gate in their attempt to reach Will Fair and, more than likely, hang him.

Jed turned in his seat as if he could feel the Sheriff's eyes burn into him. He cleared his throat, adjusted his tie only worn for church and fancy dances before he returned his eyes toward the front of the court.

Will Fair, sat with his face set with no emotion and his eyes, as they had been through the whole trial, stared straight ahead. His head high, shoulders back, he didn't even seem to be breathing.

In the very back, over a hundred black men and women stood in the Negro section. Women fanned themselves. The men, most with suits on, stood with hats in hand. Tension filled the over-crowded room.

One man, Mr. Isaiah Jones, who stood a few bodies down from the Sheriff, bowed his head and looked back up with a warm smile. He nodded and whispered just loud enough for the Sheriff to hear, "We know," he said. "We all know what you did. Won't be one day go by we aren't grateful. We're all brothers and sisters under His care."

"Amen," replied the others next to him.

"Jury," the judge said, "what is your verdict?"

The foreman stood, wiped his brow with a handkerchief, cleared his throat, and read, "We the jury find Mr. William Fair not guilty."

A gasp as soft as a breeze. A whispered, "Halleluiah," as heart-felt as a wife's love. Fair bowed his head. His shoulders shook. Jed Baker's leg shook, too. His wife placed her hand on his knee. Nothing more.

Despite how packed the courtroom was, there were no demonstrations, no threats, or violence after the verdict was announced. Not on that day or any other.

Some fumed silently around the city. They talked in darkened corners and behind closed doors, mainly when the whiskey flowed and they needed something to fuel their shallow minds. They predicted that the whole affair would be the end of Sheriff White's political career.

But the sheriff went on to serve into the 1920s, respected and revered.

"The judge was the second leader to stand up for Fair's rights to a fair trial," Debra Hutchins, local librarian at Spartanburg County Library Headquarters, reported. "What the sheriff, the jury, and the judge did at that time was heroic and historic. This was such an important case in the south. Instead of another case of violence, this person got a fair trial where evidence was examined carefully."

The actions of the Sheriff and a few others, as well as the judge and the jury showed tremendous courage in a desperate situation, and during a time of unrest when there were so many disadvantages from both the racial imbalance and civil rights.

Spartanburg's black community deemed Sheriff White a hero. A large portion of the white community also supported him. "People who followed the trial, and the whole city did, listened to the evidence and knew it was a fair trial," Hutchins said.

More than a hundred years later, the sheriff's brave act is remembered by his family as well. His integrity lives on as inspiration for his great-great nephew, Michael Smith, a Spartanburg County deputy, an investigator with the county coroner's office, and a U.S. marshal. His daughter, Lauren Smith, is a criminal justice student at the University of South Carolina.

"You think about the courage it took," Smith said. "You think about the chaos and confusion…he remembered his oath—to serve."

After the trial, Fair was told, mainly by those quiet mutters, that it might be inadvisable for him to remain in the vicinity. Fair agreed. He accepted a position at a railroad construction camp 300 miles away. He left that night.

Will Fair died in 1943 and is buried in Spartanburg's Oakwood Cemetery beside his wife and two daughters. Under the shade of an elm tree, he has a view of the court house and the jail where a brave man risked his own life to defend another and where the values he demonstrated live on.

A century later, the tale about a man who resolved to do what was right on that steamy day in 1913 is still told. It stands as the legend of a good man and his choice to respect all people, to protect their rights, to uphold his oath for justice regardless of color, race, gender, or creed.

In a time of segregation, he showed bravery and "took a stand against pressure," Lauren Smith said. Sheriff White was prepared, without thought to his own wellbeing, to act, and in that moment, changed lives.

NOTE: All names with exception of Sheriff James White, Judge George Gage, Debra Hutchins, Michael Smith, and Lauren Smith, are fictional. This is a representation of true events.

Tom Thumb

David F. McInnis, Sr.

I heard the chant of the tobacco auctioneer from my front porch, my home in front of Hugh Gregory's tobacco warehouse on Hwy 76/378 in Timmonsville.

Thousands of pounds of tobacco passed through the massive structure each week during the government regulated tobacco sales season. Representatives of all major tobacco companies such as R.J. Reynolds and American Tobacco Company began to arrive the week before the sales began. Most of these people were season regulars and well known to the community.

The growth and sale of tobacco was a big deal in the Pee Dee area of the state. The sale of the golden leaf gave each community in which a tobacco warehouse was located an economic shot in the arm.

But the most exciting part of the entire process for me was listening to the auctioneers. The chant and tone of voice from each auctioneer was distinct—a true art form. I spent many hours on hot summer days listening and observing. My father ran the hot dog stand attached to the front wall inside the warehouse. He made the best hot dogs I have ever tasted. His chili dogs with onions, mustard, and/or mayonnaise topped with relish still causes my mouth to water when remembered.

As a six year old, I helped keep ice for drinks in the cooler. The ice was delivered in 50 lbs. blocks. Another young boy and I went to work on each block with ice picks of various descriptions until it was suitable for placing in soft drink cups.

Another unforgettable thing about those warehouse days, was the smell of flue-cured tobacco. It's been more than 40 years since I have been to a tobacco warehouse during a sale, but I can recall the odor like it was yesterday. It is a smell that takes me home.

The tobacco was placed in baskets in the form of a shallow dish approximately 3ft. x 3ft. The baskets were made of woven wooden strips and each held between 150 to 175 pounds of tobacco with the identity of the farmer/seller on a form placed on top of the pile. The baskets formed long lines from one end of the warehouse to the other. Each line allowed for an aisle about three feet wide.

Down the aisles came the auctioneer followed by a warehouse representative and buyers from the various tobacco companies They moved non-stop with the auctioneer taking a cue from the warehouse rep as to what price to start the bidding on each pile. The auctioneer chanted asking for prices, and the buyers gave a hand signal when a price mentioned was what he was willing to pay. (I say "he" because there were no females to be found in this process during those years.)

The sale of each pile lasted maybe four to five seconds and was sold to the last buyer recognized by the auctioneer. The second warehouse rep would then write out the winning bid and place the bid amount and name of the buyer on each pile as they went by. If the farmer did not agree that he got a fair price for his tobacco, he could reject the bid and either sell on another day or take it to another market.

The "lugs" (bottom leaves) on the tobacco stalk were cropped, cured, and sold during the first days of the sale season. These leaves were of lesser quality and did not sell for near the price that leaves higher on the stalk. Their priced fluctuated from week to week depending on supply and demand at the manufacturing plants, a process that worked, but must have been fraught with bookkeeping nightmares.

All this took place in an environment where the temperature often rose to 110 degrees or higher. There was no such thing as air conditioning and fans were inadequate.

The whole process proved exciting and entertaining for a small boy like me who had no radio, no television, no social agenda, and who had not gotten into sports yet. I loved every minute of it.

Mr. Hugh Gregory, the owner of the warehouse, was a central figure in our town, and I was in love with his daughter, Sugarlump, whose real name was Elizabeth, the apple of her daddy's eye. He called her Sugarlump when he first laid eyes on her the day she was born. And the nickname stuck. I never heard her referred to by her given name until she was an adult.

Sugarlump and I were in the first grade together. She was the prettiest girl in Timmonsville Grammar School, and all the boys, including me, liked her. But to me, it was not important how the other boys felt about her because she and I were to become man and wife the next day. And on one particular day, Sugarlump Gregory stood in my living room. We were to be married in a Tom Thumb wedding.

At that age, I had no conception of what a real wedding was about much less a Tom Thumb wedding. I was told it was sort of like a play that churches, schools, and other organizations often held as fund raisers.

We were rehearsing in my living room that fine afternoon. My mother and Aunt Jessie Mae McInnis were in charge of the rehearsal. Our speaking lines were simple, and the best part of the whole thing was when I got to hold Sugarlump's hand. I also got to hold her arm as we walked down an imaginary aisle.

At the time, I'm sure I felt that my selection as groom was just the good taste of those doing the selecting. In later years, I came to appreciate that my selection was no accident nor was it a recognition of talent. The simple truth was that I was closest in size to the actual Tom Thumb, the hero of P.T. Barnum's, "The Greatest Show on Earth." All boys in first grade are about the same size, but I was already on the short side. (This disparity in height became more apparent at about the 8th grade.)

Sugarlump's selection as bride, however, had great merit. She was a beautiful little girl, well-mannered, and reminded me of a six year old Shirley Temple. She even had the dimples and curly hair.

On the other hand, her future groom had not yet become acquainted with hairbrushes, shined shoes, or wrinkle-free clothes. Mark Twain would have been proud of Timmonsville's answer to Tom Sawyer.

On our wedding day we finished rehearsal, and with no audience, it was a snap. But things would be different the next evening with every seat in the school auditorium full and my heart in my throat.

Outside in my yard, Hugh Gregory, Jr., waited with his goat "One Eye." The goat was called One Eye because he had a black circle around one of his eyes. One Eye pulled a small wagon around town toting the Gregory children wherever they needed to go. So, with rehearsal over, Sugarlump and I met Hugh, Jr. out front. Hugh loaded his sister into the wagon, and with me walking beside him, he delivered his sister, and my future bride, to their home two blocks away. At that point, Hugh and I were free to seek our own adventures.

Adventure was not easily found in Timmonsville in 1938, but behind the tobacco warehouse was a forest with trails leading through the vast wooded area. The problem was that all the areas looked alike, and it was easy to get turned around. Lost even.

But Hugh and I bounced happily along in the wagon pulled by One Eye, oblivious to that possibility. The wagon sported two balloon bicycle tires. These particular balloon tires were the fashion in the first half of the last century, and they were different from the balloon tires available today. Back then, they were designed to handle tough road conditions and were heavy. On top of that, they didn't roll very easily and steering was not the best.

Hugh and I had played in those woods on many occasions, but that day we ventured farther into the forest than ever before. I wasn't afraid though. Hugh Jr. was three years older than I was, and he was my hero and mentor. If he had suggested we travel by goat-drawn wagon to Charleston, I doubt if I would have argued. Especially since at my age, I had no idea where Charleston was located.

We had great fun that afternoon throwing rocks at birds, looking for lizards, and doing mostly what young boys do. But things came to a halt when Hugh asked me if I knew the way home. I didn't know exactly where I was, so there was no way I knew the way home. So we started off in one direction, only to stop and turn in another direction. I didn't know a lot back then, but I was sure we had passed the same bush and tree several times.

Finally, Hugh admitted he was lost. I had already said I didn't know how to get home, so that left only one hope—One Eye. Pulling him away from the patch of grass he munched on, Hugh and I climbed into the wagon again and pointed our navigator in the direction we had been headed. Then we sat back and left the rest up to him.

When we came to an intersection, One Eye stopped, looked, listened, and sniffed before proceeding. He did the same at each turn of the trail. As I remember, old One Eye never took a wrong turn, and after about 30 minutes, we arrived at the back door of the Gregory's warehouse.

I was glad to see it because dark was coming on. The thought of being lost in the woods in the dark didn't bother me as much as knowing the price I'd pay for being late for supper and causing my parents to worry about me. Hugh dropped me off in front of my house and nonchalantly mentioned he had known where we were the whole time. But even at six years old, I could recognize a lie.

The next evening was exciting for my family and me. A Tom Thumb wedding was a big occasion for a small town. It was a social event that brought many people together. But what had first appeared to be just another school event for me, suddenly took on serious proportions when I saw the huge crowd entering the auditorium.

Realizing I was one of the main characters they were there to see, I wished I had paid closer attention to what I was supposed to do and say. Time came to get things started, and I, for the first time in my life, experienced stage fright. Sugarlump suddenly became the strong one in the wedding party. She grabbed my hand, told me what to say, where to stand, and what to do.

Unlike real weddings, the bride and groom enter together in Tom Thumb weddings and come down the aisle arm in arm. That night, Sugarlump's arm might have been the only thing that kept me from fleeing for my life had not one other pillar of support showed up just before time to begin our march.

Dickey Knopf, my best friend and next-door neighbor, had been slightly irritated at being left out of the wedding hullabaloo. I had been preoccupied with Sugarlump and other things for the 8 to 10 days before that night and had slighted my best friend and apparently hurt his feelings.

Standing on the verge of our long walk, Sugarlump in a miniature, formal wedding gown, and I in black tie and tails, Dickey, wearing a white long sleeve shirt and blue jeans, suddenly appeared to my right.

Seeing my nervousness over the looming affair, Dickey grinned and said, "Don't worry, buddy. I'm gonna be right here with ya."

So, unknown to everyone else there, Sugarlump and I locked arms and began to march to the altar with Dickey Knopf arm-locked to my other side. Many in attendance studied their printed programs trying to find the name of the third person in the wedding party, and as we made our way down the aisle, whispers became chuckles, and chuckles became outright laughter. And just like that, Dickey "Huckleberry" Knopf stole the show.

He never left my side during the ceremony. And after Sugarlump and I were pronounced man and wife, the three of us marched back up the aisle together.

The article in the local weekly newspaper the next week gave Dickey top billing. Mark Twain would have been proud, I'm sure. Sugarlump's picture accompanied the article, but my name was barely mentioned.

Worse, I don't even remember the honeymoon.

My Third Ear

Jay Wright

I recently drove a dear friend to a doctor's office in the upstate. I thought I'd use that gift of time to work on a poem that had been struggling to get out of my head and into the big world. I made some long-awaited progress on that, but then my third ear alarm went off. It's the ear I use to listen for words, phrases, scenarios, most anything that can be crafted into my writing.

The alarm sounded when an elderly lady entered the room followed by two teenagers.   The woman's unkempt ash brown, shoulder-length hair drew attention to gray roots begging for a long-overdue color treatment. She wore a plain white peasant top over designer jeans. She directed the teens to have a seat.

Then the woman began a conversation with the receptionist. Her tone and demeanor were warm, but her volume blared above the normal conversation decibels. She explained that she was having some hearing and vision difficulties and asked the receptionist to read and complete the standard medical history papers for her.

"Sure, no problem, Ma'am."

The conversation snagged my attention away from my poetry, and the situation became a bit more interesting when the lady turned to the teenage boy and girl over by the door and said, "Y'all both just sit down sommers, and figure out where we gonna eat lunch. Right now I gotta finish up here, and y'all are makin' me nervous just standin' there like a sack o' salt and starin' at me."

"Yes, Grandmommy."

The boy went to one side of the waiting room and began texting before his bottom hit the chair cushion. The young girl went to the other side and did the same.

Grandmommy turned her attention back to the receptionist. "My two grandkids here are visitin' this week from Ohio, and all they study about is them cell phones and food. I tell ya. Grandkids. Ain't nuthin' like 'em. Lord, I've enjoyed 'em so much, but I'm ready for them to head home. You got any?"

"No, Ma'am."

By now I realized a real slice of upstate life was unfolding right before me, so I drew a line on my yellow pad under the poetry scribbles, tuned in my third ear, and started capturing their conversation.

Grandmommy handed the receptionist her driver's license, and the receptionist was writing contact information on the form.

"Okay, P – E – Y – T – O – N. Say, are y'all any kin to any Payton's over around Beaufort?"

"No, Hon. But my son's second wife was a P-A-Y-T-O-N."

"Okay." The receptionist moved to another blank space, paused, raised one eyebrow and tilted her head. "Old Schoolhouse Road? I'm not familiar with that road name."

Grandmommy leaned on the desk. "Hon, it's not fifteen miles from right here.   Remember that old Pentecostal Church that was hit by lightnin' and burned slap down to the ground?"

"No, Ma'am."

Grandmommy waved her hand forward, barely missing the receptionist's cheek. "Probably 'fore your time, Hon. Come to think of it, I believe Reagan was President. Anyhow, that's the road we live on. Next question. "

The receptionist turned to a new sheet on the form. "Ma'am, I'll read a list of things.   Let me know 'yes' or 'no' if it applies to you."

'Ever had diabetes?"

"No. "

"Okey dokey. Shortness of breath?"

"Yes."

"Okey dokey. Do you currently smoke?"

"Yes."

"Okey dokey. Consume alcohol regularly?"

"Yes."

"Okey dokey. Currently take any non-prescription drugs?"

"Yes."

While I found myself intrigued by Grandmommy's exciting life, neither grandchild was phased by her answers. Both grandchildren were still fully engrossed in their phones.

"Okey dokey."

"No."

"Okey dokey. "Ever tested positive for Herpes?

Up to this point, I'd been looking down at my yellow pad, but my head snapped up at this point to better focus on Grandmommy's answer. She didn't give an audible response, but from my side view, I could see that she mouthed "yes" while giving the receptionist a long, wide-eyed glare over the top of her glasses. The next question kept me looking their way.

"Are you currently using birth control pills?"

I watched as Grandmommy's glare became a scowl, and her posture stiffened. "Hon, *really*. God-a-mighty. "

The receptionist's head jerked upwards, and her face paled. Managing a half smile, she began shuffling the papers and said quickly. "Let's set an appointment."

Grandmommy turned to the kids and said, "Y'all decided on lunch yet?"

"We like Olive Garden."

"Uh-uh. Now, Hon, that's fancy and real expensive. Y'all need to pick something else. "

"How about Cracker Barrel?"

"Oh, good Lord, child, that is, too. Go get in the car. We'll find something. I think we passed a Wendy's back yonder on 81."

"Uhhhh …   Grandmommy …   "

"Go on, get in the car. We'll see where you take me someday when I'm visitin' and y'all are payin' for it with social security – if they's any damn such thing by then."

The granddaughter yelled, "Can I drive? He drove on the way here."

"Okay, Hon. Y'all go ahead and get in the front. I'll get in the back in a minute. "

To the receptionist: "All they study is food and drivin' and sex."

"Look who's talking, Granny," I thought

"I'll take that slot at 9:00 o'clock on the twentieth. That'll get me out of here in time to get to the wine tastin'. Hey, write wine tastin' down there on your calendar so you can remind me."

"Uh, okay, Ma'am. Here. Here's an appointment card."

Grandmommy took the card and dropped it into a huge purse. "I'm glad you gave me that, but lordy, they's no tellin' what purse I'll grab up next. Do y'all call a day before to remind us about appointments?"

"Yes, Ma'am."

"Good. Between bunco, red hats, and line dancin' with my singles group, I just can't keep it all straight."

Grandmommy and the kids left, and I was no closer to a having a poem than she was to having a clean medical history.

But I savored the story I had collected by my fine-tuned third ear. There's a story most everywhere, if you listen.

What Horse?

John Beckham

Debacle: the word clearly describes my freshman year at the College of Charleston.

The fall semester flew by faster than coeds doing shots, which was a large part of the debacle. I not only incurred the wrath of my parents over my grades, but the school and the fraternity I was pledged to weren't very impressed either. This was 1985 and C of C was entering the height of its "cocktail college" reputation.

With party after party being thrown at me, my studies were constantly barraged by distractions, not least of which was my like-minded girlfriend Blair, who, although she had equally partaken in those distractions, somehow managed to squeak the minimum grade needed to become a sister in her sorority. After several stern lectures from my parents, friends, and fraternity, I made a promise I would turn over a new leaf and stay focused.

Spring semester arrived and crept by slower than a calculus lecture. I was off to a rocky start. Midterms came and went. I found myself staring at the real possibility of serious academic trouble. I was worried, and Blair could see this. I begged off several invites to parties where she and I normally would have gone together, so it was understandable she was frustrated with me. Our relationship took a hard hit. The pressure grew.

"Look, I think I have a solution to your anxiety," she said one day. "What you need is the Carolina Cup."

The Cup, as it is affectionately called, is the most anticipated event of the year for all colleges in South Carolina. This Camden steeplechase heralds in the beginning of spring where the ladies wear Laura Ashley sundresses and wide-brimmed hats. The gentlemen wear the basic southern uniform of khakis, an oxford, a tie (loosened of course), loafers, and Ray-Ban or Vuarnet sunglasses. As we get older, the seersucker suits and bowties come out.

Row after row of cars, trucks, tents, grills, and tables line the infield as people meet up to eat and drink the day away. Flags flying the Gamecock or Tiger colors can be seen everywhere and college students who drink beer all day eventually start hobnobbing with the older, bourbon drinking men. Football disagreements are argued, resolved, and the competition continues.

Where some attendees may have a spread of deviled eggs, casseroles, and ham biscuits, others may have a simple box of KFC. I held a partiality to Yogi Bear's honey-fried chicken from Hartsville, SC. I've yet to find better in the state. Heaven is swimming in a pool of that delicious damn chicken.

In spite of the fact that the Cup is a horse race, one of the long-standing catchphrases of the event is "I Never Saw a Horse." The crowds are so large, and the partying is such the focal point that few people go to the Cup for the actual race. But the underlying truth for many is even had we ventured close enough to the actual track to see a horse, we most likely would not remember.

So, Blair and I agreed to attend to help relieve my tension and worry. We stayed with friends in Columbia and planned to convoy to the race. Blair decided to drive. The day was expectedly filled with drinking, flirting, laughing, etc.—the classic Cup experience.

No relationship is perfect, and ours certainly wasn't going to be the first, and sometimes when Blair and I took the train to Boozetown, we began to get on each other's nerves. The spats were so insignificant that the causes of the disputes were rarely even memorable. Such was the case at this particular Carolina Cup. I don't know why we were arguing; I don't know what started it, but we left the Cup in a fight that continued as we drove back to Columbia.

Bearing down I-20, I had enough of whatever the fight concerned and decided to play the let-me-out-of-the-car card—usually the best bluff in my hand. Unless she calls it. She did.

"I'm going to get out." I said.

"Ok," she replied, pulling over to the shoulder, a beautiful smile on her face.

I opened the door and stumbled out. "I'm getting out…" I drawled.

"Bye!" She punched the accelerator, the car door slammed shut, and I was staring at my girlfriend's tail lights as she sped away.

Blair had literally dumped me.

I consoled myself with the thought it would only be a matter of time before she turned back. They almost always sometimes usually maybe do. The problem was I couldn't see an exit down the road, so I was going to be waiting a while. And along with that realization came a grand idea: I would hitchhike back to Columbia.

Blair would turn around to come back for me, but I would be gone. She would panic. She'd maybe think I had been abducted. She'd feel *terrible* for putting me out!

Now, along with these brilliant thoughts came the assumption that one of my friends would see me on the side of the interstate, pick me up, give me a ride back to Columbia. Blair would be so freaked out when she couldn't find me, that by the time we met back up at our friend's house, she'd be soooo relieved I would win the argument by default. Whatever the argument was.

But after a few minutes on the side of the interstate with no friends to the rescue, I decided to thumb it. Great idea, I know... but with my thoughts hazy, it seemed the thing to do. I couldn't let Blair return and find me waiting for her. So I cocked my knee and stuck out my thumb, and sure enough a car slowed down to pick me up.

I looked to see which of my friends it was... and... it was... a Dodge Dart.

Hmmm, who owned a Dodge Dart?

The passenger's window rolled down. A pretty woman leaned out.

This might be interesting, I thought.

I leaned down to better take in the view. A man sat in the driver's seat. He was a dead ringer for Matthew McConaughey from *Dazed and Confused*. The woman resembled Diane Lane from *The Outsiders*. This was a good-looking couple.

But I didn't know them.

And they were in a Dodge Dart.

Matthew leaned over and asked, "Hey frat boy, you need a ride?"

Frat boy? This was a very astute observation to make of a stranger hitchhiking down I-20.

I chuckled and gave my winningest smile, hopefully deterring them from any ideas of abduction and murder. "Actually I'm just a pledge…"

"A what?" Diane said. "Where you headed?"

Stuck in the predicament of explaining I'm waiting for a friend to pick me up before my girlfriend has a chance to come back sounded stupid, so I settled for simplicity.

"Yeah, I'm just trying to get back to Columbia…"

"Well, jump in!" Matthew said before I could finish.

So I did. My new, irrational logic was that I would catch a ride with these two surprisingly attractive rednecks and surprise my girlfriend. Or they would kill me, and she really would be sorry, and then I'd win the argument by default.

Whatever the outcome, I climbed into the backseat thinking the two in front wouldn't be able to pull a knife or gun without me seeing it first and rescuing myself.

Matthew took off down the road and turned his head toward me in the back. "I gotta get this girl home to her husband first. It's getting late. So we're going to make a quick stop."

Of course, this is how the story of my disappearance begins I thought. "Oh so you two aren't a couple?" I smiled at him in the rearview mirror, trying to be polite.

"Naw," Matthew said, "We're just friends. Me and her husband go back a ways."

Diane laughed, leaned over, and kissed Matthew on the neck. She lifted a bottle to her mouth, but Matthew took it from her and passed it back to me.

"Here ya go, take a pull on that. She's had enough." He handed me peach schnapps. I admit I was shocked. *Peach schnapps in a Dodge Dart trying to get back to my baby...* BOOM... country music. Was that how songs are made? Was it that easy?

I eyed the schnapps like a kid who'd been handed candy from a stranger in a van. "So just drink it straight from the bottle?" I asked.

They both laughed. Diane sidled up closer to Matthew in the front seat. If we were headed to see the husband, I sensed there could be trouble. She was deep in the sauce and wasn't afraid to flirt with Matthew.

I leaned back and took a few swigs off the peach schnapps. It was disgustingly sweet yet smooth and comforting at the same time.

Matthew continued to drive, and I saw daylight dwindling. I also noticed something odd. We were passing *through* Columbia. Feelings of impending murder returned.

"Where exactly is this husband of hers?" I asked as calmly as possible.

"Irmo," he says.

"Ah," I say. "That explains why we just left the Columbia city limits."

For the first time Diane turned around. "She's so pretty," I thought, wondering what she was doing with…oh! She tried to smile coyly, but Diane had not taken advantage of modern-day dental care. Ever. Her teeth looked like someone stuffed firecrackers in her mouth and sewed her lips shut.

"You ain't in no hurry are you?" she asked.

"Nah," I said, trying to sound indifferent. I turned away and took a few more swings of the schnapps. It was quickly becoming my pacifier. I hugged the bottle with a grip that could have choked a giraffe. Mixed with the other alcohol I had consumed at the Cup, I began to feel more resigned to my imminent death.

The next minutes found me swigging on more schnapps; Matthew pushing an ever more flirtatious Diane away, and Diane getting more rambunctious. Finally Matthew pulled off the highway and quickly exited into the gravel driveway of a mobile home park.

Dusk had settled in, and the orange and purple glow of sunset hung over the trailer park like the closing curtain on a bad play.

I wondered how panicked Blair was, confident she had indeed turned back to get me. She would have made it back to our friend's house by now, I thought. And she had probably called all over checking if anyone had seen me. She might even have worried I'd been picked up by some rednecks. She might have thought me dead.

But the peach schnapps told me I didn't care. *You have to die of something, right?*

The Dodge Dart came to a stop in front of a trailer that was modeled after Pisa, leaning over on crumbling cinder blocks, a nearby rusted grill fallen on its side to match the streaks of corrosion and grime that covered the roof and exterior. Some lights shone from inside, but the filthy windows blurred the images inside. Or maybe it was the schnapps.

Matthew told me to wait in the car while he and Diane went inside.

Some kids ran around the dirt yard, and a few other people milled about, moving closer to the Dart trying not to be obvious about looking to see who I was.

I decided not to be trapped in a Dodge Dart when the natives came for me, and I surely didn't want my family to have to identify my body in a Dodge Dart, so I climbed out and leaned on the door. I thought I surely looked like a local—only one that happened to be wearing an oxford shirt, a tie, sunglasses, and loafers.

The kids stopped and stared at me. Another guy a few mobiles over looked up from working on his motorcycle. Yep, I was definitely fitting in.

Sounds from inside the trailer left no doubt that quite an argument had started up. The trailer shook a bit, and some serious cussing was afoot. The distinct sound of a pot or pan hitting the wall teetered the trailer even more precariously.

I imagined Matthew and Diane's husband fighting, or maybe Diane and Matthew killing the husband and deciding where to hide the body. Which I thought better be in the trunk because I was calling dibs on the back seat with the bottle of peach schnapps.

A loud slap pierced the thin walls, shaking some grime from the windows. Seconds later the trailer door burst open. Out came a six-foot-tall, balding, paunch-bellied man wearing a "wife-beater" shirt, a spot-on match for tall Danny Devito.

Diane's husband, of course.

I would have thought Danny had done very well for himself marrying Diane or that Matthew was a better match for her. But the teeth on Diane...what a mess.

Danny rubbed his stubbly jaw and then turned to see me standing just a few yards away. I've seen drunken angry eyes before, and this man certainly had them.

Danny yelled at me, "And just who the fuck are you?"

"Good evening, sir!" I held up my pacifier bottle of peach schnapps.

Brilliant, I know.

"Is that my damn peach fuckin' schnapps?" he asked.

I sighed. Of course it was.

The door to the trailer flew open with a bang. Matthew ran out, pushed past Danny, and aimed for the Dodge Dart.

"Get in!" he yelled.

I looked toward the trailer and saw Danny wobbling, but still on his feet. His eyes never left mine. I wondered where Diane was.

"I'm going to kill your ass frat boy!" Danny yelled.

What was with all the frat boy comments? And why kill me?

Oh yeah, the schnapps.

I opened the car door and started to get in. "I'm just a pledge!" I yelled back at Danny.

"Screw Diane," I said to Matthew. "Let's go!"

Matthew sprayed gravel as the Dodge Dart bee-lined for the exit of the trailer park. All the natives threw their support with Danny, merged into one giant yelling crowd around him, and yelled at us.

When we got on solid asphalt at last, Matthew asked, "Who the hell is Diane?"

I just grinned, realizing the names were just in my head. A very fuzzy head.

"What happened in there, man?" I asked Matthew. But he didn't want to talk about it so the ride back to Columbia was a quiet one. I figured most of it out myself anyway. But I did wonder about Diane and if she'd be ok. Then I assured myself she was the type who could take care of herself.

Several hours after Blair had left me stranded on the interstate, Matthew took me to a bar near the Williams-Brice stadium, the only landmark I knew that was anywhere close to my friend's house.

We didn't have cell phones back then, and I didn't know exactly where my friend lived, so I had to use a phone book and pay phone at the bar.

Matthew hung around for a bit, but then took off without even saying goodbye.

My friend answered the phone and wanted to know what had happened. He thought I was dead and had been calling everyone to see if anyone had seen me on the highway.

"It's a long story," I told him.

Blair was on the way to get me. She actually had been frantic, he said. I'll admit that made me happy.

When she finally found me in the bar, we hugged. Apologies from both sides followed. I hadn't actually won the argument, but it felt sort of like I had at least drawn a tie.

At my friend's house, I discovered I still held onto the bottle of peach schnapps. It was empty, and I have no idea when I finished it off.

"So, how were the races," my friend asked, eyeing the empty bottle.

I grinned and winked.

"Don't know. I never saw a horse."

A Day's Journey

Martha Greenway

"Life is a journey and not a destination"
~Lynn H. Hough

It was early spring and my friend Myra and I decided to drive the twenty-five miles from Sumter, South Carolina, over to Bishopville. I wanted to find the topiary garden I had read about.

These were the days before GPS and cell phones, so upon arriving in Bishopville, we pulled into the Exxon station to ask directions. A big man pumped gas and looked friendly.

"Excuse me," I yelled out the car window, "Do you know how I'd find Pearl Fryar's garden?"

"Yes, ma'am, I do," he said with a smile, "He's my neighbor."

And, just like all good southerners, his directions were, "Turn around and head back yonder way—like you was going back to Sumter. Watch for the Hardee's on your right but don't stop there...the best burgers are back off Main at the Dairy

Queen. You need to turn right onto Broad Acres Road, but make sure you don't turn before, or you'll end up in the town cemetery."

Bishopville is a small town (its population is under 4,000), but even I didn't expect the man putting gas into his car to be Pearl Fryar's neighbor. We easily found the incredible topiary garden on Broad Acres Road, and, yes, it is fabulous. But we will get to that story in a moment.

Leaving the gardens, I spotted a van, literally covered in cameras, parked beside the "Welcome to Bishopville" sign. Excited, I asked Myra to pull over. She stayed in the car, but I hopped out and approached the young driver of the van.

"Y'all not from around here are you?" I said.

"No, we're from California." He introduced himself as Harrod Blank, a filmmaker and photographer from Berkeley. I had heard about him. His father, Les Blank was a well-known independent documentary film maker who mostly filmed musicians, but the local university had recently held a showing of his film "Burden of Dreams"—a documentary of a documentary— about the filming of Werner Herzog's "Fitzcarraldo".

"We're here to film the Button King," Harrod Blank continued. Blank told me he had dreamed about a van covered in cameras that cruised the country taking candid photos of people who stopped to stare at the camera-encrusted van. He awoke and began to fulfill this dream. The Camera Van has its own website http://www.cameravan.com/ and has crossed the country many times, as well as making appearances in England and Germany. Blank also wrote a song titled "The Camera Van Song."

Dalton Stevens, the man Blank was seeking, is known locally as the Button King. Stevens couldn't sleep one night, so he decided to sew some buttons onto his clothes. He continued the activity night after night. Before he knew it, he had completely covered his jacket, trousers, and hat with buttons.

He went on to cover a coffin, a Chevrolet Chevette, and even a toilet with buttons. He lives just a little outside of Bishopville and converted an old barn into a museum/meeting house. On Friday nights there's always a pot luck while he and friends play some good old country music.

"Well," I advised Mr. Blank before leaving, "you also need to talk to Pearl Fryar, the Plant Man."

Before my first visit to his garden, I met Pearl at Patriot Hall where the Sumter County Cultural Commission sponsored a visual arts exhibition called "Out of Necessity: Art Driven by the Soul." It featured paintings and sculptures created by artists using the means available to communicate and express feelings, dreams, and concepts.

In Pearl's case, it meant creating a magical topiary garden using plants discarded and left to die by the local nursery. He created amazing shapes out of shrubs that had rarely, if ever, been used in topiary. From sasanqua camellia to cedars, firs, holly trees to pines and junipers, Pearl's mathematical mind led him to trim those plants into geometric shapes—beautiful squares, boxes, triangles and pyramids. One of his signature works is a tall Leyland cypress, trimmed and trained to a fishbone design.

But Pearl didn't stop with discarded greenery. He also created sculpture from bits and pieces of discarded metal objects, clay pots, or used printing plates from the soft drink canning company where he worked. One of the sculptures he brought for the exhibit had the words "Love and Unity" on one side and "Hate Hurts" on the other. I would learn through the years that this man who carved out "Love, Peace and Goodwill" in the grassy part of his garden really lived those philosophies.

A couple of years later, Pearl worked with hundreds of high school students to create a mosaic garden in a vacant space off Main Street in Sumter.

For several years, he was artist-in-residence with the art department of Coker College in nearby Hartsville. One of his large topiaries was transplanted to the grounds of the South Carolina State Museum in Columbia and smaller pieces of his sculpture are in their collection. Nationally and internationally known in gardening circles, he is a sought-after public speaker.

Pearl once told me he didn't know he was an artist until we invited him to be a part of "Out of Necessity" and called him one. He is a man who sees fountains and sculptures in materials most people throw away. His imagination, hard work, and God-given talent nurtured a garden so remarkable it draws visitors from around the globe. To affirm to him that, yes, he is an artist was one of the highlights of my career.

Harrod Blank later showed up throughout the country at art car shows. The Button King showed up in Blank's film, "Automorphosis." Pearl Fryar showed up in the documentary "A Man Called Pearl," and I showed up in Pearl Fryar's garden dozens more times.

The Camera Van, the Button King, the Plant Man—all in one afternoon in Bishopville. Whew! What a day it had been.

Earmouths

Ryan Crawford

While working in the hundred-degree South Carolina heat, I often find myself dreaming of outer space. It's cold there, I hear. And quiet.

From a rooftop one can hear the amassed reverberations of every passing car, every working machine, every screaming or crying or laughing mouth. It could, in a more delicate ear, coalesce into a symphony. But for me, it is discordant and mean: territorial fights, wars over parking spaces, a sale at the supercenter. The expanding noise lacks the inherent rhythm of nature. And yet, when I'm up there, I find a peace I've been unable to find anywhere else.

This job came along like most events in my life—with no effort on my part, no ambition. My grandfather had the insight or the dumb luck to invest in satellite dishes when they first came out and were used chiefly in the commercial market. He had an electronics store that was barely scraping by until he began selling televisions. The store was then able to take in a decent profit, and it steadily prospered. He opened a branch in Anderson, another in Greenville.

Then the satellites were cast out, caught like bits of trash in orbit, and my grandfather thought that was the most amazing thing. They became his obsession.

Then as now, anything separated from the planet seemed magical because it, unlike us, had been able to escape. Most of us experience moments of suffocating agitation, the feeling of being squeezed in by people and buildings and machines, knowing that—outside of moving to a remote desert or jungle—there's no escape from them.

Imagining something floating all alone, quiet and cool and free from the press of gravity, is a quick trip to nirvana. What if I was sound? What if I was light? Every now and then I needed something like that. It kept me in a weird kind of balance. It was the same for my grandfather.

My father worked at the main branch of our stores in Due West with my grandfather. He said the old man talked about satellites nonstop. When I was younger, my father took me to the shop, and I'd listen to the two of them while picking through the treasure of odd parts in the back repair room, trying to put together a picture of satellites floating in space and the beams they threw down and scattered around the planet.

"All these signals from beyond the atmosphere," my grandfather said in his husky singsong, the watch on his wrist rattling as he moved his hands. "And it becomes data, pictures, sound. That's the future, Danny." My father's name was Dan; only my grandfather called him Danny. "And you and me are right smack in the middle of it."

And they were. My grandfather learned all he could about the operations of satellites and ordered the dishes and other equipment. He wanted to get into data transfer because he thought that was the easiest way to make money. He imagined all the convenience stores and restaurants and hotels that would begin using these things, and he wanted to be their supplier. In five years he was one of the top five major distributors of commercial satellite dishes in the Southeast. Then business picked up enough for my grandfather to buy a bigger house and put in a pool and get a new truck. And my father was in line to take his place.

We were a family of dreamers. I dreamed of finding a little cabin in the woods where I could be left alone and make stained glass windows. My grandfather dreamed of a future-land empire. My father's dream was a bit more conventional.

He had always wanted a Harley. I could tell when he was dreaming about it. We'd be out on the porch drinking sweet tea. When we knew my mother wouldn't be around for a while—maybe she was washing Sunday dishes or away at the grocery store—he would take out his silver flask and pour a little bourbon into our glasses. It wasn't the alcohol that made us so happy about that, it was just that he had done it. It was one of those harmless things that the people in our small town would get huffy about, and we liked sticking our tongues out together.

Then we would just sit there, not talking—my father and I never needed to talk and that's why we liked hanging out with each other—just sitting there listening to the birds and the wind in the trees and feeling the cool of the concrete porch on our bare feet as the warmth of the sun buzzed in everything.

The Harley dream was his nirvana, in a rocking chair with a cold glass of spiked sweet tea in his hand, looking out to the buzzing grass without seeing it. His happiness made me happy. We had a rare and precious symbiosis on days like that that had nothing to do with family or even being human. It was just that we were away, together.

When the store started taking in money from the satellite dishes, my grandfather decided to buy my father a bike. We all went together on a Saturday afternoon. At the door of the dealership, I could see stirring just beneath my father's skin— effulgence—a childlike wonder, delight, and disbelief. When we walked inside, his lips began to tremble beneath his dark mustache. It was beautiful how he, *even he*, couldn't keep it together. The way he ran his fingers over those creamy cool bodies. I knew he would've killed somebody to have one if the dealer told him he had to.

The one he'd always wanted wasn't there, so he had to special order it. It was a pearl FXRS Low Rider Special Edition. It was delivered two months later, and I rarely saw my father after that.

Never had I imagined something as simple as owning a motorcycle could change someone so. He lost weight, looked ten years younger. This once gruff and tempered old man held himself like a prince, with all the pep and hauteur he could muster in his shoulders. He bought a leather jacket and an intimidating pair of black boots.

While getting a snack late at night, I could see, in the light of the open refrigerator, the eagle keychain glowing from its hook on the wall. Before the sun was up, I knew it would again be soaring over the tarmac.

We don't know exactly what happened, but I imagine he was living out that porch dream. He opened her up when no one was on the road. As he gained speed, I imagined ropes of tears, like transparent streamers, torn out of his eyes in the wind. It was something he never thought he would have, that Harley, and there he was with it, gripping, being.

Then a green Dodge Ram came around a corner. I never saw it, but that's what was written in the paper. A green Dodge Ram I imagined droning like a massive June bug as it whipped into view. The man driving had been drinking. Everybody wanted me to get mad at that man. They wanted me to get up in court and work the judge and jury into a sympathetic vengeance, get the man locked away for the rest of his life.

How, I wanted to scream at them, "Is that going to make anything better?"

I didn't appear in court, and others might hate me for saying this, but I wish that man well. He didn't want to kill my father. He was just trying to have a good time, maybe had gotten some really good news or really bad news, and he made a big mistake. He went to jail for a little over a year. He'll either learn from it, or he'll keep making more mistakes, and eventually he'll die or be locked away again.

What do I have to do with that? It's going to balance itself out one way or another on its own. Human or not, the inherent rhythm of nature will eventually out. I couldn't say any of that to my family or friends, of course, because they would have stopped wanting to talk to me. You get really honest with folks, and they'll turn on you every time.

All I can do is imagine that my father kept on riding right through that truck, leaving the accident, the road, his body lying there held down by laws, and him riding off weightless, those streamers fanning out behind, along a perfect, endless road. I'll look out to a star sometimes and think about how far away it is, and I know he'd already ripped past long ago, his stretched palm having smacked the side of it as he passed by—the viscosity of time—my eyes just now catching that stirred up flame.

So now I'm in line to take my grandfather's business, and he's got me apprenticed by doing what we call de-installs. That's when one of the old, big-as-a-whale's-contact-lens dishes comes down and is replaced with new tiny ones. Everyone wants to do it because it looks nicer, and they say there are new satellites up there in space now or that something's been changed about the old ones, so the new dishes work better. I don't know if there's any truth in it, but people want them changed anyway, and that's more business for us.

Anyway, I take the big dish apart and throw it down to the parking lot. Then I climb down for the new dish and carry it up, install that, and that's it. All together it usually takes me about two hours, and I walk away with a hundred-fifty bucks for each job. These numbers accumulate into the vision of my cabin in the woods.

To me, the dishes look like ears. That's how I see them, as ears listening to some secret from space, then seamlessly transforming to mouths hollering the news from Earth. Earmouths. It has an alien quality to it.

I can feel the satellites buzzing when I've got them in place. I used to use this digital tool that could read when the signal was strongest, but now I can feel it on my own. The feeling is like thinking you can feel an earthquake coming when there isn't one, if that makes any sense.

I often sit in front of the dish for a while after I have it up. Just sitting there with my eyes closed. Feeling it. Imagining all the space and atmosphere the beam passed through, all the birds that flew through it like that beam was an invisible rainbow. Sometimes, if I sit there long enough, I believe I can pick up the information being transmitted—numbers and images spontaneously appear in my head—and sometimes I can—I know I can—hear my father's bike.

Previously published in part in *Torpedo Volume 3*, 2008, subsequently published in the anthology *Torpedo's Greatest Hits* (Melbourne, Hunter Publishers, 2009).

Sock Dancin'

Sandy Richardson

"Do you believe in hell?" Rhett Butler asks Scarlett in *Gone With the Wind.* She tells him yes because she was raised on it. Well, growing up in South Carolina as a child and grandchild of true believers, I was raised on hell, too.

To reinforce the threat of fire and brimstone for eternity and to provide a firm righteous foundation, I inherited a great many warnings, including those about the evils of whiskey, the sins of gambling, and dangers of sex before marriage. I also understood about hell on earth from the stories my grandparents told me about life during the Great Depression. These were not religious warnings about sin; instead, they were first-hand accounts of a time when locusts and dust storms and bread lines were the order of the day. These were true horror stories.

As I grew older, those hard-times stories stuck with me. I'm certain they were filled with the exaggerations, superstitions, and colorful embellishments most Southern storytellers are known for. And while I now can question some of the information, in my childhood, I believed and loved those stories, and I made my grandmama tell them over and over—especially the one about Sammy Lee.

Sammy Lee was a wiry little man with big calloused hands, bowed legs, and dancing feet.

During the Depression years, he worked odd jobs around town: plowing gardens, butchering pigs, building fences. And in the cotton season, Sammy Lee worked down at the cotton gin where he handled the big shoot that sucked the cotton right out of the wagons and then spewed it out into the huge metal bins to be packed down and baled. That shoot swung back and forth over the bins all day long.

And while those storms of cotton whirled around and down, Sammy Lee sang his two favorite songs: "Come and Search My Big Fat Pocketbook" and "If Ya Wanna See Yo Mama, Ya Gotta Meet 'er in the Sky."

By the end of the day, Sammy Lee, hoarse and sweaty, left his job covered in cotton lint. It clung to his clothes and stuck in his eyebrows and eyelashes, but he never seemed to mind—especially on Fridays, because after work on Fridays, Sammy Lee got to do what he loved best. He'd take himself straight home, bathe, and change, and then head back to town.

The children loved Fridays, too. They gathered on the sidewalks downtown every week and played marbles or jacks while they waited for Sammy Lee. Near dusk dark the lookout would shout, "Here he comes. I see him coming!" Then the children scrambled for seats along the roadside to watch as Sammy Lee sauntered up in high style.

He arrived dressed in black trousers, a starched white shirt, checkered suspenders, and his shiny, black, dancing shoes. And riding high-up on his shoulder was Jambo.

Jambo was a French-Algerian monkey, and how he met up with Sammy Lee nobody really knew, but the two lived together quite happily, and both enjoyed this Friday night ritual. Jambo dressed for it, too. He sported short pants, a red vest trimmed in gold braid, and a black pill box hat with a gold tassel on one side. Around his wrists, wide elastic bands held two tiny, silver cymbals in place, so he could clang them together.

Once the two of them arrived, Sammy Lee laid his big leather satchel on the ground and from inside of it, took a dented tin cup which he handed to Jambo. The little monkey then scrambled down Sammy Lee's arm and went from child to child with the cup, shrieking every time a penny clanged into it. Afterwards, he put the cup back in the satchel and climbed on top of an old wooden crate, clanging his tiny cymbals together.

When the children grew quiet, Sammy Lee blew a few notes on his harmonica; Jambo clanged his cymbals, and the show began. Jambo twirled and somersaulted on top of the crate while Sammy Lee tapped danced and soft-shoed his way up and down the sidewalk. The children clapped and sang along, and then when they couldn't keep still any longer, they danced down the street behind Sammy Lee.

The adults often gathered to watch and leave jars of pickles and canned vegetables for Sammy Lee. After all the singing and dancing was done, Sammy Lee handed the leather satchel to Jambo to pass out lemon drops or peppermint candy to each of the children.

Candy was a rare treat in those days of the Depression, and Sammy Lee used the pennies he collected from the children one week, plus some of his own meager earnings to buy candy for the next. For several years, that candy was the only treat the children got, and Sammy Lee's music and dancing brought the people of the town a brief and welcome respite from the harshness of their lives.

But as fate would have it, one Friday night, Sammy Lee and Jambo failed to arrive as usual. The children waited; the adults came; but no music and laughter broke the night silence. The sheriff and two men decided to ride out to Sammy Lee's place to see what had happened.

The men drove up the rutted dirt drive to the small shack nestled in a grove of oaks on the edge of town. When they stepped from the car, they saw Jambo dressed in his dancing

suit and huddled on the edge of the window sill. But there was
no sign of Sammy Lee.

"Sammy Lee! Sammy Lee!" the men called. But there
was no answer.

The three men walked onto the porch and through the
open door to the inside of the house. Jambo screeched and
chattered nervously as the men checked first the front room and
then the back room but found them empty.

Opening the back door, the Sheriff peered out into the
dusky light.

"Here he is…back here…he's hurt," he shouted to the
other men.

Sammy Lee lay sprawled on his back across the narrow
porch, one leg sunk deep into a hole in the rotted boards. His
head lay catty-cornered across the top step and hung awkwardly
over the edge of it. A blotch of red stained the collar of his white
shirt and blood had dripped and pooled onto the second step.

"I'll go fetch the doctor and get back as soon as I can,"
one of the men said, but the sheriff motioned for him to wait.
He knelt and put his hand on Sammy's chest. He put his ear
close to Sammy's mouth, and then looked up at his friends and
shook his head from side to side.

"Even if you could magically fly the twenty miles there
and back, the doc can't do no good. Po' soul has done danced
his last dance."

The sheriff studied the hole in the porch floor and the step where Sammy Lee's head rested. "Must've come out here for something,' turned, and then stepped through that rotten board. He went backward and hit his head right there," he said, pointing toward the corner of the step. The other men nodded in agreement.

"Let's get 'im inside and covered up. I'll go 'round and tell his pastor." The sheriff shook his head again and motioned for the men to help him. They carefully lifted Sammy Lee's frail body. When they did, Sammy Lee's head slumped forward onto his chest, revealing a blood-soaked shirt back and a gaping wound at the back of his skull.

Solemnly, the men laid Sammy Lee gently on his narrow cot. With great respect, the men covered his body with a worn cotton sheet and turned sadly to catch Jambo and take him back to town. But when the sheriff tried to pick him up, the little monkey gave a loud shriek and jumped through the window, escaping into the thick woods behind the house. The men had no choice but to leave him on his own for the night.

Now, because morticians were extremely rare in the rural areas during those days, and also because the weather was so very hot and humid, it was decided that two women from the church would bathe and dress Sammy Lee's body the next morning. The men would bring the coffin out, and the funeral would be held in the afternoon.

Even on such short notice, nearly everyone in town showed up to pay their last respects. The few stores in town closed; the cotton gin shut down, and mourners filled every pew and aisle of the little chapel on the other side of the woods from Sammy Lee's house.

One by one, the people filed by the open casket to say goodbye to the little man who had spread such joy and happiness in the community. He looked so fine in his starched, white shirt, black jacket, and striped bow tie, but he did not look like the Sammy Lee everyone remembered. Sammy Lee had never been so still or so silent. And, of course, he did not have on his dancing shoes.

As the last person filed past the casket, two somber deacons began a slow march toward the front of the church. It was time to take Sammy Lee away. The gentle notes of "Amazing Grace" swelled to fill the small chapel. Women and children sobbed. Men blew their noses, and----- a cymbal clanged?

Yes, it was a cymbal! And leaping through the open window came Jambo scrambling towards Sammy Lee's casket and beating his little, silver cymbals as hard as he could.

The deacons rushed to grab him, but before they could, Jambo lurched forward and landed right on Sammy Lee's chest. There atop Sammy Lee's crisp, starched shirt the monkey jumped up and down three times and beat his tiny hands together, until… *Glory Be To God!*

A great sucking-in of air sounded as Sammy Lee sat straight up in his coffin.

Children screamed.

Men gulped.

Women fainted.

As for Sammy Lee, he took another deep, loud breath and climbed out of that box. He perched Jambo on his shoulder and grinned at everyone. Then he danced in his socks right out of that church.

Legacy

Dale Barwick

All the men in my father's family hunted. The tradition spanned the generations of our family to the time when hunting provided the only way to put meat on the table. By the time I came along in the early '60s, many things and ways of life, including people, had changed in the South, but my daddy's wasn't one of them.

Raised during a time when women didn't wear pants, much less camouflaged ones, it didn't occur to him to take me hunting. Perhaps he thought a girl couldn't keep up, would make too much noise, would become bored, or would get upset at the sight of a dead animal. But each time he flung open the kitchen door after a hunt, rubbing his cold hands together and smelling like the sweet woods, I longed to go where he had been.

One afternoon when he picked up his gun, I followed him into the yard.

"Please, Daddy, please. Take me with you."

Either he felt uncharacteristically patient, or my brown, puppy-dog eyes persuaded him. Daddy took me quail hunting that day. I walked behind him quietly and placed my feet in his footprints.

Reb, our brown and white English Setter, crisscrossed the field ahead of us, nose to the ground and in the air, occasionally looking back at my father's hand signals for directions. At times, all I could see of Reb was his feathery white tail moving through tall brush. When he neared the edge of the woods, he slowed, perking his ears. He froze, front leg up, tail straight out.

"Careful....Careful," Daddy crooned to the dog in a low voice as we crept closer.

Suddenly, a wild thunderclap of wings erupted around us. Before I could cover my ears and gasp, Daddy swung his shotgun to his shoulder.

BOOM!

He strode quickly to the area where the quail fell. "Reb, hunt dead. Dead. Hunt dead in here."

The dog's tail wagged as he sniffed the area where Daddy pointed. He found the dead bird, gently picked it up, and delivered it into my father's outstretched hand. Daddy slipped it into the pouch of his hunting vest, rubbed Reb's ears, and gave him a soft slap on the ribs.

"Good boy!" And we were off to find the singles which had flown into the nearby woods.

The hunt that day turned out to be the first of many. In time, Daddy taught me how to clean the quail, doves, and ducks he killed. He showed me how to pluck feathers and how to use a candle flame to singe off any remaining down. We used kitchen shears to split the carcasses in half. I watched, fascinated, as he named the organs – heart, liver, gizzard, and craw.

Occasionally, as he pulled out the entrails, his face twisted, and he held his breath for long stretches of time, blowing out hard and sucking air back in through his pursed lips. I didn't ask why.

The first time we cleaned a deer together, Daddy's reaction was even worse. He hooked a steel spreader bar between the deer's hind legs and hoisted it with a rope. With the deer hanging head-down, Daddy skinned it with a knife, beginning at the tail, pulling hide away from flesh as he worked his way down toward the neck.

But, after he put the sharp tip of the knife into the deer's nether region and split the carcass down to its throat, Daddy heaved. Then when he cut through to internal organs, he retched and turned his head aside to vomit. I hid my astonishment as I realized that my strong, tall daddy was squeamish.

The next time he cleaned a deer, the same thing happened. When the organs splashed onto the ground, Daddy retched, and I couldn't hold back a belly-laugh. He looked at me with a mixture of sheepishness and irritation.

"What?" he growled. "This doesn't bother you?"

"No, sir…I kinda like the guts."

"The smell doesn't get to you?" he asked. "That's what gets to me. The smell."

"What smell? I don't smell anything but blood," I said with a giggle.

"Well, come here, then," he said, handing me the knife. "You do it."

To my father's surprise, I enjoyed skinning and eviscerating game and getting sticky blood and guts on my hands. I loved it as much as walking through the woods, scouting prey, hiding in camouflage, watching dogs work, and feeling my heart race the second before a gun exploded.

But, even though I enjoyed shooting guns at targets, I never wanted to kill an animal. I was content to let Daddy do the killing while I cleaned the quarry, garnering an admiration from him that always amused me. We made an interesting pair: a grown man too squeamish to gut a deer and a young girl too tenderhearted to pull a trigger.

My father died a few years before his namesake, my son, Will, was born. Will came into this world a hunter. Because of his early fascination with guns, I gave him his granddaddy's shotgun before he was big enough to lift it. Throughout his childhood, I told him stories about going hunting with my daddy, and we watched hunting shows together.

When he was about six, Will went on a duck hunt with my husband. Afterwards, I taught him how to dress the birds. Like me, he was fascinated with the internal anatomy. He quickly learned to clean any quarry without help.

He hunted at every opportunity. Even during the off-season, he practiced. If he wasn't shooting at targets, 'he shot squirrels. He practiced his duck and turkey calls to the point I banned him to the yard with them.

When he was twelve, a long-awaited turkey hunt was called off the night beforehand because my husband got sick. A very disappointed young boy went to bed.

A few hours before dawn, I woke to a gentle, yet persistent tapping on my arm.

"Hey, Mom, will you take me hunting?" Will whispered into the darkness of my bedroom.

I sat up in bed, hoping not to wake my sick husband. In the light of my bedside clock, Will's puppy-dog eyes, so like mine years before, begged me to take him.

"You want *me* to take you?" I whispered, realizing that it hadn't occurred to me to offer.

"Didn't you used to hunt with your dad? You can still do it, can't you?"

"Shhh. Don't wake your daddy. Let's go to your room and talk about it," I said, thinking that I might be able to convince Will to go back to sleep.

But in the light of his room, I saw he already wore his hunting clothes. The hope in his eyes had turned to excitement.

Still trying to dissuade him, I said, "I don't know how to use a turkey call."

"Mom, I know how to do everything. All I need you to do is to drive."

"But I don't have anything to wear," I said. I hadn't owned hunting attire since my daddy died.

"You can wear some of my camo. Please, Mom, please," he said as he pulled his youth-sized pants and shirt out of a drawer and handed them to me.

Still wearing my nightgown, I pulled on the camo pants. They fit me perfectly. Will and I grinned, and I began to feel an excitement I hadn't felt in years.

On the way out of town, Will explained where he wanted to set up the decoys and where we would sit. He demonstrated the two turkey calls he planned to use, a mouth call and a scratch call. He told me how to use the camouflage mosquito netting, and he reminded me that turkeys were skittish, so I shouldn't move even if a mosquito found its way inside the net.

As we pulled onto the dirt road of our farm, he said, "Mom, turn off the headlights. Turkeys are real smart, and I don't want to scare them off. We can't use a flashlight either, so you'll have to let your eyes get used to the dark. Just follow me, and don't talk. I'll show you where to sit."

Per his earlier instruction, when I got out of the car, I closed the door noiselessly and stood still for a few minutes to let my eyes adjust to the dark. I followed Will into the woods, carefully placing my feet where he stepped to avoid cracking twigs and rustling leaves.

About fifty yards into the woods, he pointed to an oak and motioned for me to sit. He set up three turkey decoys in a clearing as I settled on the ground. We leaned against the big oak and waited in the cool April pre-dawn.

Crickets chirped, frogs croaked, and hundreds of mosquitoes buzzed around us and crawled across the camouflage netting over our faces. As the stars faded from the sky, Will placed a yellow turkey call in his mouth. "Key-yuk, key-yuk," he called, patiently waiting.

The boy who couldn't sit still in a classroom didn't move a muscle for over an hour. About the time my legs grew numb, an answering gobble came from the trees in front of us.

I spotted the turkey about thirty yards away. Will shifted slightly, calling to the gobbler. Before I could cover my ears and gasp, he pressed my Daddy's shotgun to his shoulder. BOOM!

He put down his gun, whooped at the top of his lungs, and raced toward the felled turkey.

"Mom, look! He's humongous!" he called as he held the bird upside down by the feet, pointing out to me the beard and spurs. "This one's going on my wall."

"Nice job. I had no idea you could be still and quiet that long. I loved it!"

"Really? I didn't think you wanted to come. Did you really have fun?" he asked with a surprised look on his face.

"Yes, I really did. I'll take you hunting any time."

Will grinned.

So, now our family legacy continues through Daddy's daughter to his grandson, a hunter who would make our ancestors proud.

An Ordinary Life in Extraordinary Times

Annette Reynolds

"This time on our glorious planet is the most exciting time in history.
We are going to see and experience the impossible becoming possible,
in every field of human endeavor and on every subject."

(*The Secret* by Rhonda Byrne)

Both my parents were alumni at S.C. State College (now University) in Orangeburg, SC. When I got my acceptance letter to attend, we went down to the school to talk with the band director, Mr. Reginald Thomasson. Daddy did all the talking.

"Reggie," Daddy said, "Annette has a skill and that must be compensated."

"C.C., no majorette has ever received a band scholarship," Mr. Thomasson answered.

"She is not a majorette, she's a twirler—the first twirler this college has ever had. If you want her on the band, she must be compensated like any other band member." Daddy was adamant.

I won the required audition for twirler handily as at the time – 1965 – black girls were not allowed to attend twirling camps. The band tried to put 100 members on the field, so the name could be The Marching 100. That year, my freshman year, the band had 100 members and me. It was named the Garnet and Blue Marching 101 Band. My 15 minutes of fame: I was the One.

Ah, freshman year in college: a great time. I thought I would be a majorette/twirler. I didn't know I would be Annette The Majorette. Free of Daddy and my younger brother and sister, an excellent student, The Majorette on a marching band scholarship, finally able to date – no such thing at home. Perfect. Perfect for my family's finances, too. Daddy negotiated again and got a second semester presidential scholarship because I was an asset to the college. I don't remember whose idea that was, but Daddy knew a lot of people at the college. He was always preaching 'be an asset not a liability.'

My sophomore year, I was surprised when my 1965 picture in twirler uniform appeared in the February 1966 issue of Ebony Magazine. The issue's title proclaimed "Black Girls Are Getting Prettier" and featured students from several different black colleges.

That same year, three things happened that would send me on a different trajectory. I got married (secretly so I could stay in the dormitory), and I became pregnant. Then on February 8, 1968, I experienced my first encounter with the racism my family and the segregated Black community tried to shield me from.

I was studying in the library that night. Just before the library closed, I walked outside and saw students, mostly guys, walking toward the front campus. They carried what looked like small tree limbs. The number of people present was unusual, so I stopped two people I knew, Sam (Hamilton) and Larry (Hathaway), and asked what was going on. They thought a bond fire was being built.

We decided to stand in a little park-like area among the trees in front of White Hall for a little while. Then Sam decided to go where most of the students were "on the hill" to see what was going on. He was going to come back, and I guess we would have gone our separate ways afterward.

And then, Larry and I watched as shots were fired, and fellow students fell to the ground. I heard a big boom after my friends fell, then several pops, and people yelling, "Stay down!"

From behind me, Larry screamed, "Run, Annette."

My feet had already taken flight, and I headed for Bradham Hall. I lived off campus by then, and the dormitory was closed for the night, but the house mother let me in anyway.

I ran to the back of the dormitory to the TV room and watched as students were carried, dragged, and helped into Brooks Infirmary.

What was at first called a riot happened around 10:30 pm. The 11:00 pm news reported "All's well in Orangeburg."

The other girls kept asking me what happened, but I couldn't talk, couldn't tell them. I was trying to process how and why.

We were not allowed to make any calls on the only phone in the dormitory and stayed in the hall on first floor all night, terrified, wondering what would happen next. The next morning we lined up at the pay phones to call home. When it was my turn, I called my husband. When no one answered, the operator said when I hung up the phone would be out of order.

"Wait," I said and gave her my parents' number to call.

Daddy told me to go home and pack what I could if I could and meet him between Bradham and Manning hall in two hours. When he arrived, several of my school mates were waiting with me to go back to Darlington. We piled into the Daddy's station wagon.

I sat in the living room that night with the TV turned on. Mama came in the room, turned the TV off, and said, "You don't want to watch that."

But I don't even remember what was on TV that night, maybe a western. It was then that I realized silent tears were streaming down my face. Mama held and rocked me like the child I was.

I never told my parents where I had been or what I saw. I didn't know the students that died—Sam or Smitty—we were just school mates. I didn't know the high school student at all. I did know the students didn't riot and that was later documented in a book titled *Orangeburg Massacre* by author Jack Bass.

And I did know it could have been me—shot dead.

Later that semester, my presidential scholarship was cancelled. I thought, well, a married mother of an infant probably isn't what you want representing the college as the twirler. I no longer considered myself an asset to the college, and my 15 minutes of fame were over.

I didn't bother to ask if my assessment was true because my husband forbade me to go back to S.C. State. I grieved for my friends, but he claimed it was too dangerous after the riot, and we needed to work on the marriage.

My father-in-law said, "Why don't you apply to Limestone College?" and laughed. It was really a smirk, but I didn't catch it. I didn't know what or where Limestone College was, but I knew I had to finish college to be a 4-H Agent. So when I was alone, I looked in the phone book and found a listing for the college.

I dialed the number, and my first question was "Do you have a Home Economics program?"

Answer: yes.

This was a blessing since there were only three colleges in the state with that degree.

Second question: "Where are you located?"

The college was in Gaffney, SC, where we lived, but on the other side of town. I didn't think about how I would get there or how I would pay for it. I simply completed the application mailed to me, included the required picture, and requested my transcripts from State.

Then I waited. I told no one.

My husband and his family didn't believe it when I told them I had been accepted. My husband said no Negro was allowed on that campus. Even my father was adamantly opposed to my attending and ordered me to go back to S.C. State. But I pushed forward.

Attending Limestone proved first a culture shock, and then a culture shift for me. Limestone is the third oldest college in South Carolina, the first women's college in the state, and one of the first in the nation for white women. It has a long reputation for producing excellent graduates.

It would be delusional to think any success I had was the result of my being extraordinary. The simple truth is I worked hard, really hard, and I had help from others like everyone who succeeds. Daddy accustomed me to hard work.

On the day that I arrived at Limestone College, all I saw was a sea of white faces. They all looked the same, and I could not distinguish individuals. However they were friendly and welcoming which helped me relax.

Mrs. Ruth Lane, my advisor helped me with my master schedule. She was a jewel as an advisor and as an instructor. And even though the campus was small, I still had to learn my way around. The other students were very helpful. If there were students who didn't want me there, they did not come near me. There always seemed to be friendly students around me, and most of my instructors treated me like any other student.

There were a couple of difficult instructors. One said the class was full and would not let me register for it. When I asked Ms. Lane for help she wrote a note, placed it in a sealed envelope, wrote the instructor's name on it and instructed me to deliver it.

I was able to register for the class after the note was read. The instructor ignored me and would not call on me even when I raised my hand. Being ignored by a white person was not new to me, and the subject we studied wasn't new or that hard to me either. So I managed okay.

The other instructor that proved difficult told me I would sit up front beside the teachers' desk because "you people cheat." However, when I came to class the next time, she had changed her mind, and I was allowed to sit with the other students. I understood that some of the students reported what she said to the administration. She became more polite, but still made it difficult for me. Not being able to ask questions and get clarification from the instructor meant I had to work harder. Ms. Lane assigned me a tutor who really helped. I managed to earn B's in both classes.

There were no threats or other unpleasantness. Definitely no shooting. But I couldn't say the same for my home life.

I couldn't study or work on homework assignments in the chaos I called home. When offered a work-study job, I chose the library, and that is where I completed and left my homework.

I even gave a passing thought to changing my major to library science because I love to read and love being surrounded by books. I had loved going to school since the occasional times I went to the two room school where my parents taught.

But I stayed focused because at home, my marriage had deteriorated into domestic violence.

Graduation day finally came, and I earned my Bachelor of Science degree in Home Economics. Just as important, I became the first African-American graduate of Limestone College!

Not graduating was not in my vocabulary as I decided to be a 4-H agent in 5th grade. My parents came to the ceremony, but my husband did not, and it wasn't long before we were divorced.

In 1975, I became an alumni of S.C. State like my parents by earning a Master of Education degree. I enjoyed a 30 year career with the Clemson University Extension Service beginning as a 4-H agent in 1970. I retired as Cluster Director of Beaufort, Colleton, and Jasper Counties in 2000.

The 60's made the impossible possible for many: the Civil Rights Movement and Women's Movement that made way for the Battered Women's Movement changed many lives for the better.

Along with my career with the Extension Service, I also worked in the Battered Women's Movement as a survivor of domestic violence. Survivors helped establish shelter programs all over the United States, and I wrote a book about it: *Survivors Thrive.*

I still consider myself an ordinary person living in extraordinary times. My mother saw transportation change from the horse and buggy, to the car, then to the airplane and even to the spaceship, all in her lifetime. I have seen the invention of radio, television, and computers in mine. Because of the telegram, telephone, and cell phone as means of communication, we're now connected at a grassroots level around the world. We can participate in efforts toward the common good no matter where we are or what our cultural background. We are one human family, humankind—not black, white, yellow, nor red-skinned. Rather, we are all different shades and tints of brown.

> "The wrong in the world continues to exist just because people talk only of their ideals, and do not strive to put them into practice. If actions took the place of words, the world's misery would very soon be changed into comfort. A man who does great good, and talks not of it, is on the way to perfection. The man who has accomplished a small good and magnifies it in his speech Is worth very little."
>
> The Baha'i Faith

I was an ordinary person drawn into extraordinary circumstances. But hardship can prepare an ordinary person for an extraordinary destiny. Maybe it is good not to know what we can't do, so we can walk the spiritual path God lays out for us.

We live in extraordinary times. For the first time in history, everyone can view the entire planet. This makes world peace not only possible but inevitable.

Believe it or not the world is less violent now than any other time in history. I believe that when each of us focuses on the good in the world, it helps us all find our path on the road to peace.

Mr. Samsonite

John Beckham

A few years back, I lay in bed around eleven on Thursday evening, reading a book and about to call it a night as I had work the next day. The phone rang, and it was my buddy Pete wanting me to meet him downtown Charleston. Right then. At 11 p.m. He's was with a girl from work and another girl from the Columbia office. He needed me to be the fourth wheel.

"No way," I said. "It's too late. I have work in the morning, and I'm tired."

Then he played his trump card, "You owe me."

I did. And he knew it. This wasn't something I could get out of with my honor intact. One of the most important parts of the guy code is being a good wing man, and you always return the favor of being a wing man. Pete was calling to collect. I had to go.

I lived on James Island, a fifteen-minute drive, but ten minutes later I sped downtown using my usual repertoire of cuss words and some I reserved for special occasions. I really did not want to do this.

Pete was in real estate and networked all the time. That night a few other agents had arrived from Columbia for a meeting. They had been drinking for a few hours at a work function and were just hitting their stride at Coast restaurant, a place known for its famous mojitos and past-hours drinks.

Pete and his friends were excited to see me as most drunk people are when they coax someone new into their web of debauchery. They waved me over from their perch at the end of the bar. Everyone was laughing and being loud and trying to hook up. Everyone except me. I really did not want to be there.

Pete introduced me to Sadie and then abandoned me for the end of the bar where he and a lady friend were stationed. Sadie was pretty sauced, and immediately I found she was pawsy—the type who needs to put her hand on your arm or shoulder to have a conversation.

I want to go on record saying she wasn't unattractive. And it's not like I wasn't interested in meeting someone. I just wasn't in the frame of mind to play catch up to a bunch of drunks, so I could get on their level. My plan was to just grin and bear it.

But twenty minutes of listening to Sadie put me in hell's misery. She only talked about real estate and unleashed a barrage of insults at every estate agent and client in the greater Charleston and Columbia metro areas. I gave her points for her colorful insults and originality, but the whole conversation grew tiresome as drunk, negative, sweating women can often be at midnight in July and when the listener is stone-cold sober.

She droned on about market rates, her hand resting on my arm, and suddenly, I had a brilliant idea. My thoughts shifted to making the best of this situation. I wasn't going to start drinking at midnight, and I realized, I didn't ever have to see this woman again. So I could be whoever I wanted to be. I could say anything. I could be the world's worst wingman.

I decided to lie. And since I was going to lie, I decided to do it audaciously.

I leaned over to her and said what gets every woman excited, "Can I tell you a secret?"

Her eyes grew wide, and she licked her lips with greedy interest.

"Absolutely."

"I feel sorta bad," I said with a hangdog look. "You see, Pete doesn't know this... no one does... but I feel you're someone I can trust."

I had her full attention.

"What is it?" she asks.

"Don't tell Pete, but I've met someone. I've been dating her pretty seriously for the last couple of months."

She raised an eyebrow and nodded. I continued. "But it's awkward because she's from California. And rich. Really rich. She's the heiress to the Samsonite luggage fortune."

"Wow," Sadie said.

"And I'm glad I've told you because I want a woman's opinion on something." She nodded again.

"You see, she asked if I might be open to something." I stalled, looking around the room, really playing the part.

"Yeah?" Sadie pressed impatiently.

"Well, California is a different place, as you know, and she asked if I would take her last name instead of her taking mine. What do you think?"

"You take her last name? That's kind of weird..."

"I know!" I said, "I would be John Samsonite."

"Wait... what?" The puzzled look on her face was priceless.

"Exactly! I thought the same thing! Samsonite is actually the last name of the family who owns the company, not some made up name like you would think. I think it must be Russian or something. How crazy is that?"

"That is really crazy," she said, totally confused. I could see her brain trying hard to make some sense of this. I sensed some sort of warning sounding off in her head like a muffled echo. But watching her face, I saw the booze win and drown out the warning with: "We are so drunk! Woohoo!"

"So should I give in? I mean if I keep my name her dad might get mad." I don't give her a chance to answer. I'm on a roll. "But I'm pretty sure he's going to die soon anyway. Let's hope, right?" I laugh and elbow her in the ribs.

Her face changed a bit, not liking what I had said. I leaned in even closer. "If you really want to know the truth… I'm totally marrying her for the money."

"WHAT?!" she yelled.

"She's decent looking and all, but I have to be honest with myself. Would I be interested in her if she wasn't worth millions? I have to say 'no.' Gotta keep it real, right?"

"That's horrible!" she said.

I try to look offended. "Really? You think so? I mean… women do it all the time."

"No we do not!" she said, defending her gender.

"What's the big deal," I asked, "We'll probably get divorced in a few years. I get half the money. Move back to the South. She finds someone new. Everyone wins."

Her paw pointed at me. "You're a bad person! I don't like you!" She started to turn around, but I caught her by the wrist. It was my turn to play pawsy.

"Hey, listen if it makes you feel any better, leave me your card. I'll call you when I'm looking to buy a house. It'll be big. South of Broad big."

"You're a ducking bass pole," Sadie sputtered in all her righteous tipsiness. She slid off her bar stool and stumbled away from me.

"Hey, I'll even throw in some luggage! And remember, don't tell anyone!" I shouted at her back.

I sat by myself and watched Pete rushing over. As a wingman, I'd pretty much crashed and burned. But at least I could head back across the Ashley and catch some rest.

"Hey, what was that all about?" he asked.

"I have no idea. She's hammered. But hey," I slapped him on his back, "good times, man. Call me again next time y'all go out."

Pete looked from me to his date across the room. Standing beside her, Sadie was in full hand-gesturing, cussing mode. But Pete was pretty tight, himself, and the confusion was too much for him. I clapped him on the shoulder and turned to leave, smiling. By the time he returned to his seat and heard Sadie's story, I'd be long gone.

Come to think of it, I haven't talked to Pete in a real long time. But I think of him and Sadie every time I pack my Samsonite suitcase.

The Footnotes: Story of a Beach Band

Johnny Hilton

"This Magic Moment"

Going to the beach. These words possess both magic and mystery for most South Carolinians. A beach trip is part of the culture of our state, passed from one generation to the next. Our grandparents and our parents did it; we did it, and our children will do it, too, because the stories we heard as little kids about beach trips made back in the day were the stuff dreams are made of.

As little children at the beach with our parents, we play in the sand and surf. But kids grow into pre-teens yearning to be old enough to make the trek on their own for a different kind of play. The first trip to the beach during high school is a rite of passage teenagers in South Carolina cherish. House parties during spring break and the first week of June are plunges into rushing waters spiked with freedom and the chance for romance. Once in college, the trips come more often, and a spur of the moment road trip is a sure thing. The ultimate passage to heaven, of course, is getting a summer job at the beach.

The breakers and salty air bring out antics that wouldn't happen back home. Going to sleep is almost out of the question as one is afraid of missing some excitement in the wee hours. And the surf, sand, and suds are a combination destined to bring on a party. It's made many a mama worry about her daughter.

On top of the brew and the sea, there's something else in this mischievous mix—music and dancing. Imbibing, music, dancing, and the ocean air have a hypnotic effect, and they can blur one's judgment.

The clubs and pavilions along the Carolina coast in the 1920's and 30's created an environment similar to that of a petri dish, allowing dance and music to sprout and grow quickly. Like brother and sister, the music and the dance developed side by side.

Beach Music sprang from Rhythm and Blues played and sung initially by African American musicians. The Shag, a dance whose history is often debated, has an unclear origin, but is claimed by many. With a shuffle beat and a shuffle step, and one's free hand positioned as if holding a cold can of beer, the movements of The Shag are smooth and cool so as not to spill a drop.

Beach clubs and pavilions thrived at all the Carolina beaches. Though often destroyed by hurricanes, new structures always replaced those lost to the wind and waves. Music and dance flourished at Roberts Pavilion, Myrtle Beach Pavilion, OD Pavilion, Pawley's Pavilion, Folly Beach Pier, The Pad, and The Barrel, just to name a few from back in the day.

"Bring it on Home to Me"

Good things always spread quickly. The music and dancing from the joints at the beach moved inland. No longer just at the beach, kids brought it back to their hometowns. The Shag and beach music invaded the parties and gatherings of folks far from the coast. This rhythm and blues music, known as R& B, evolved and grew into genres known as "soul music" and the "Motown Sound" in the sixties.

Before long, that music found the back country a hundred miles from the coast, and we small town high schoolers loved it. Of course, we tried our hand at playing it. There were lots of bands and combo's in those days. Groups formed, broke up, and formed new musical alliances.

The Footnotes had just such a genesis. The band was born in 1967, when members of two former groups, The Jackstones and The Villagers, joined forces. Tommy James, long time keyboardist and band leader of Second Nature bestowed the name The Footnotes upon the band.

Initially, The Footnotes played around Sumter at parties and often at the Teen Age Canteen, a venue sponsored by the city where middle school and high school kids gathered and danced on Friday and Saturday nights. But in short order, the band was playing at clubs in the area like the Casarena Lounge out near Shaw AFB.

Not yet old enough to buy a beer ourselves (legal age was 18 in those days), we provided the musical backdrop by which others chugged their brews. Renowned for its hard charging partiers, the owner of the Casarena had been known to discharge his hand gun into the ceiling to break up unpleasantness.

As word spread of our group, we began to travel a little, often playing out of town for various events. We played at a club in Greenwood, SC, the story of which gives a real exposé on the music and its impact on society at that time.

As mentioned earlier, the music of The Shag and the beach were based on Rhythm and Blues, with the vast majority of the recording artists being African Americans and the listeners and Shaggers being white. The Footnotes experienced the reverse when we traveled to Greenwood and performed two nights in a club where the patrons were all African Americans. We white boys played black music for a black audience and had a fantastic experience. As is always the case, music is the universal language, breaking down barriers, building bridges.

Word of The Footnotes soon reached the coast. We hooked up with a would-be agent and promoter from the beach. Unfortunately, he was a little shady, and we had to chase him down through the Horry County Sherriff's department to collect some of our performance fees. Shortly after that, however, a big break came when we got a call from the high priest of Beach Music events, Cecil Corbett.

"Down at the Beach Club"

Located on Highway 17 between Myrtle Beach and Ocean Drive, the Beach Club, operated by Cecil and Charlie Corbett was the Mecca for big name bands on the Grand Strand of South Carolina during the sixties and early seventies. The gigs we played at the Beach Club as an opening act and as the back-up band for many of the great headliners were the means by which The Footnotes came into our own.

Our first job at the Beach Club was with Billy Stewart. Sadly, some of his band members had been killed in an auto accident. This left him without a band for his engagement at the beach. The Footnotes got the call. Excited and a little nervous, we came into the club early in the afternoon to set up for rehearsal. At rehearsal time, two very large men and a lady walked up to the stage. They sat down on the front row and asked us to play some of Billy's songs.

At that point, we weren't sure which of those big guys was Billy Stewart. We found out in short order as one of them climbed onto the stage. He took the bass from the bass player and proceeded to show him the way he wanted the bass part played. When he began to sing, we all burst into smiles and could hardly contain ourselves. The sound coming from that big man's mouth was incredible.

The gigs at the Beach Club usually lasted a week. Playing every night allowed us to get our sound tight and together. After we finished a week at the Beach Club with an artist, when they returned the next time to our area, we were usually chosen as their opening act and back-up band in other venues across the Carolinas and Georgia as well.

Other great performers we worked with at the beach and other venues around the Southeast included Jackie Wilson, The Drifters, Major Lance, The Coasters, The Marvelettes, The Tams, The Platters, Archie Bell, Arthur Connelly, Lee Dorsey, Carla Thomas, and Clifford Curry.

Beach music venues included the Coachman and Four in Bennettsville, SC, The Po Boy Club in Timmonsville, SC, The Cats Eye in Raleigh, NC, The Cellar in Charlotte, NC, and Williams Lake in Sampson County, NC.

When folks heard us playing with these well-known artists, they wanted us to come to their hometown and play some music for them. These gigs at the beach club and other venues led to many jobs playing for fraternity parties and private events. Auburn, The University of Georgia, Georgia TECH, University of North Carolina, University of Virginia, University of Tennessee, and the University of South Carolina were some of the college campuses at which we performed.

And let's not forget Clemson. As the opening act for Jerry Butler in the old Field House, we performed for a packed house. People wall to wall had to be a violation of the fire code. Drinking and dancing were the order of the day. The clubs and frat parties ran wide open, full speed ahead.

Once when we backed up Billy Stewart at the Wrightsville Beach Club in North Carolina, we had a near miss with a beer bottle that was really a political commentary by a patron of the club that evening. Billy was singing "Together," originally recorded by the Intruders in 1967.

Near the end of the song, Billy liked for the band to bring the music down, so he could talk a little about racial harmony and how being "together" was a good thing. That night in Wrightsville one of the fellas in attendance tried to engage in the discourse and share with Billy his differing point of view. When Billy countered the guy's argument with his own views, we had to duck.

During the sixties and seventies, there were many needed societal changes happening in our nation, which resulted in things getting better for all of us. Thankfully, that night there was no harm done, and the show continued without further incident.

Our band members attended high school and lived in Sumter when The Footnotes came together. After graduation, we lived in a variety of places going to college or working. We drove from different directions and met at the gigs. Often we met a little early, so we could work on new material. After the gigs, we always returned home as staying overnight was more costly. We saw the sunrise many a morning after traveling all night heading home from gigs all over the Southeast.

On one occasion, several of us were traveling together actually coming back to Sumter. One of us would usually stay awake to help the driver, but on that trip, somehow we all went to asleep, including the driver, unbeknownst to the rest of us. When we awoke, it was daylight. We found ourselves almost, but not quite, off the side of the interstate. A sizeable portion of the equipment trailer stuck out in the right lane of I-20.

We were lucky that night as we often were, like the time we returned from Johnson City, Tennessee, crossing the mountains after an ice storm. We encountered an 18 wheeler jack-knifed in the road. When we stopped, our van and trailer slid toward the edge of the road and the cliff below. We jumped out and literally held on to the van and trailer for dear life, somehow managing to stop its slide off the slippery road and into the abyss.

Even with all the crazy things that sometimes happen in a traveling band, we wouldn't trade those times for anything. Just kids in our late teens and early twenties, we had the time of our lives. But all good things must come to an end, as they say. So it was with The Footnotes. We disbanded in 1971.

But fortunately, the break up was not forever.

"Reunited and It Feels so Good"

In the spring of 1999, we received a call from Hank Martin, long time South Carolina musician and friend of the band. An event was about to be held to benefit the Swan Lake Iris Gardens in Sumter. Hank called to ask about the possibility of The Footnotes getting together and playing at the benefit concert to be held in the gardens.

Initially it looked as if conflicts would prevent some of us from participating in the concert. But miraculously, at nearly the last minute, the door opened as a result of some cancellations. For the first time in 28 years the "last eight" members of The Footnotes that were in the band when we broke up, would all be in the same place at the same time. We had all remained friends over the years, and many had continued to play music, but we had not all been together at one time since our last gig 28 years previously.

We made arrangements to rehearse the afternoon of the gig at Swan Lake and climbed on the stage all together again.

The feeling of that reunion rehearsal was a powerful reminder of how music, friendship, and love can transcend time and space.

The gig that night was pure magic. We weren't nearly as polished as we had been back in the day, but the feeling on stage and the response from the audience made the few slip ups we made seem insignificant. We had such a great time and the response from the audience was such that we knew we had to do this again. Just like the Blues Brothers, we were "on a mission" to get the band back together. And we did.

We rehearsed and people began calling on us to perform: a class reunion, a local club, a birthday party. We were getting our chops back and having a blast. Every time we climbed on stage, it felt almost like we were 19 again. Soon The Footnotes were playing at wedding receptions, rehearsal parties, debutante balls, tailgate parties, and many other private events.

Then in September of 2001, we received a call that really sent us into orbit. The Footnotes had been tapped to be inducted into the South Carolina R&B and Beach Music Hall of Fame.

The actual induction took place October 27 at the Spanish Galleon in Ocean Drive, now North Myrtle Beach. Governor Jim Hodges attended the ceremony and wrote in a letter to the band "beach music has become recognized worldwide as a unique and enjoyable musical art form. All South Carolinians join me in thanking you for using your God-given talent to advance the delightful sounds of this great genre of music. "

What a thrill that was for us. Unfortunately, the R&B and Beach Music Hall of fame is no longer in existence, but we are most grateful for the recognition we received at that time.

After that event, our engagements really picked up, and we traveled more. As older men with greater commitments to family and career, the pace became a little much for some of our "last eight" members. We were faced with some personnel changes which occur in all bands. We faced many during our younger days as well. We have been fortunate over the years to have had the opportunity to work with some really first class musicians.

"Still Crazy After all These Years"

These days our gigs are somewhat calmer than and not quite as wild as some of those back in the day, but they are still exciting.

It is true there are not as many ladies dancing on table tops as before, but The Dying Roach and The Gator do still occasionally break out on the dance floor near the end of the evening. We've also seen a groom or two get really excited when singing the Delbert McClinton song "Giving It Up For

Your Love" down on one knee to his bride, feeling happy, really getting into it as if he were ready for the wedding night events to begin immediately right there in front of the bride's mom and dad. The singing down on one knee is engineered by the band, and of course, the band always hopes for something wild and crazy to happen.

I vividly remember the night a couple years ago when we did a wedding reception in Athens, Georgia. We were playing under one of those big white tents in the bride's mom's back yard. A terrible thunderstorm came up with frightful lightning and thunder. The rain poured down in buckets. A torrent of water rushed under the stage, and then the power went off all over town. Sirens screamed and fire trucks rushed everywhere.

With power off in the church during the wedding ceremony, the couple said 'I do" by candlelight. When the wedding party finally showed up at the house, they were a little shaken, but we were all determined that the show must go on.

Our guitar player and lead singer walked out on the dance floor and sang the first dance song unplugged, standing right next to the bride and groom. In the meantime, someone managed to buy a generator, which gave us enough power to run the PA and the amps allowing us to crank it up. The party turned into one of the best ever.

And speaking of wedding receptions, they and debutante balls are two of my favorite gigs. Near the end of the evening, the band invites the bride and bridesmaids or all the debs up on the stage and asks their moms to join them. So we have these middle-aged moms, dressed to the nines, wearing their finest jewelry, all while each woman shakes her booty and sings at the top of her lungs "Ride Sally Ride." Being a part of that moment is priceless!

Even as most of us in the band approach 70 years of age, we are still playing beach music and having a great time. Wedding receptions, class reunions, debutante balls, tailgate parties, and private events are our mainstay these days. We have always tried to stay true to our roots, sticking with a repertoire of rhythm and blues and the sounds of the beach. And when the dance floor is full of Shaggers, well… then we know all is right with the world.

Footnotes personnel over the years: Kenny Bell*, Randy Gleaton*+, Hugh Hodge*, Steve Mims*>, Steve Morris*>, Gene Nelson*, Rick Paulus*+, Mike Rogers*+, Bert Taylor*>, Johnny Hilton>, Charles Stafford #, Amy Whitaker#+, Mark Bradley#, Johnny Few#, Bob Fowler#, Tom Ross>, Hampton Cobb#, Leonard Brunson#, Darby Erd>, Kevin Floyd#+, Cleve Edwards#, and Bryan Hatfield>

*original member   # former member   >current member   + deceased

The House Painter

Brenda Remmes

The old house in the low country needed work. And oh my, wouldn't her relatives be impressed. It may not be a mansion on the Battery, but if not the location, the size and history were equal.

Built in the mid 1800's, six columns vaulted up three stories over a grand piazza that could accommodate sixteen rocking chairs: eight on each side of the twenty-two steps that were girdled between Nandina bushes. Over time, the limbs had become so heavy with berries the massive shrubs bent almost to the ground creating an appearance of deep red across the front foundation.

The family home had hummed with activity for eighty years, filled with ancestors who farmed the land. But the next generation moved to the city and wanted efficient heating systems and air conditioning. To install and maintain these modern conveniences in the old house threatened to be too costly. An agreement to rent out the place until somehow the money became available was the only consensus everyone could reach.

For thirty-two years an assortment of tenants came and went, each less desirable than the previous. And after three decades, the old place had been so pillaged and abused no renters appeared. Such a waste of a once majestic home. As far as Merrilee was concerned, it was time to correct this travesty. She had the mindset, and even more important, now she had the money.

Merrilee sold her condo in Charleston and retired to family land. She bought out her other cousins' share, hired an architect, and proceeded to shore up the foundation, replace the windows, gut the kitchen, create a downstairs bedroom and add a full bath.

A good year later when the carpenters and plumbers, floor sanders, and electricians had gone, she chose to employ a single man to paint the outside as well as the second floor of the house inside. He came highly recommended as an artisan who practiced his trade with attention to detail and respect for the integrity of the wood. He was not easy to schedule, and Merilee waited him out until he could fit her into his prior commitments.

His appearance surprised her. Old and bent, he climbed out of a truck similar to his own condition, both of which would have embarrassed her to be at her entrance. Opening the door, Merrilee looked momentarily baffled. The fabled artisan hardly reached as high as her chin and smelled of tobacco and whiskey. She hesitated long enough for him to notice her confusion. He started to turn.

Then Merrilee spied the name on his truck and flung open the screen. "Mr. Lattermore," she said, "I'm so glad you're finally here."

He raised his forefinger to his temple in acknowledgement and entered. Almost immediately she saw his brow furrow.

"Anything wrong?" she asked.

"We'll see," he said and walked to the middle of the foyer surveying the walls around him. "What do you want done?"

"Well, the outside, of course. It's a demanding job, let alone for one person, but I'm told you're the man."

"It'll take a while," he said. "A few months."

What she expected.

"Upstairs on the second floor," she said. "the walls haven't been painted in…well, I'm guessing more than fifty years. They will require a good deal of scraping, I'm sure."

"Upstairs?" He eyed the stairway in front of him as if calculating the number of steps he'd have to climb on a daily basis. "No renovations up there?" He'd obviously taken in the significant remodeling on the first floor.

"No," she said. An apologetic smile stretched from side to side. "I needed more of the comforts downstairs, but wanted to keep the second floor true to the original appearance."

"Then, let's take a look," he said.

He had limited mobility. As she led him up the steps, she began to have second thoughts. *This may be too challenging for him. Why had no one forewarned her?*

As if he sensed her uncertainty, he stopped midway to catch his breath, but then hunched his shoulders and pushed onward. Once in the room at the top of the stairs, he examined the various swatches of colors she'd assembled and scraped pieces of paint off the wall. The flecks crumbled at his touch, more than ready to be relieved of their responsibility. "A lot of moisture in the wood," he said. "Unusual considering the age."

"Will that be a problem?" she asked. Another budget item to include, she feared.

"Maybe," he said. "We'll see."

Merrilee entered the second room. He stopped in the doorway. "What happened in here?" he asked.

"Happened?" she said. "I'm not sure what you mean."

"It's cold. So much colder."

"I hadn't noticed," Merrilee said. "Perhaps one of the vents isn't working. I'll have it checked."

He shrugged and proceeded to the third room and finally to the bath which he examined with the same deliberate attention as the first. "It'll take me about four weeks inside," he said. "Three to four months for the outside."

"Fine," she said, as of yet uncertain how he'd ever handle the exterior, but others had convinced her he could. "When could you start?"

"I'll start tomorrow," he said as if that should be obvious.

The following day he returned with paint cans and brushes, sealers and buckets, primer and tape, and one ladder. After agreeing to his estimate, Merrilee offered to help him unload, but when he declined, she retreated to the kitchen, unable to watch his labored climbs back and forth to the second floor. Once all of his equipment had disappeared upstairs, she heard nothing. Eight hours later he descended without a word and disappeared in his truck.

This routine continued for four days, and then on the fifth day, he mysteriously didn't show up for work. After a sixth workday with no sign of him, Merrilee worried that perhaps he'd become ill. She phoned. "Mr. Lattermore," she said. "I hope you're okay. I've missed you."

A long pause greeted her.

"Yes ma'am. I need to tell you I won't be able to do your job. I'd be grateful if you'd bring my things down from the second floor and leave them on the front porch. I'll be by to pick them up." He added quickly as part of the apology, "I won't be charging you for the work I did during those four days."

Merrilee was stunned. "You're quitting?"

"Yes, ma'am, I'm afraid I am."

"Did I do or say something to offend you?"

"No ma'am, not at all. But you didn't tell me about the old lady on the second floor. I can't work with her around."

"Old lady?" Merrilee asked. "What old lady?"

"The one who keeps walking in and out of that second bedroom."

He's been drinking, Merrilee thought. The silence grew between them until finally she said, "Mr. Lattermore, there is no old lady on the second floor."

He snorted. "Maybe you've seen her, maybe you ain't. But I saw her every day, and she got under my skin. She's a mean one. You need to bring in one of those big companies with four or five people. Let them bang around and make a lot of noise. Maybe she'll leave them alone."

Merrilee hung up the phone and slowly walked to the bottom of the stairs. For a long time, she glared up half expecting to see someone glaring back. Feeling slightly silly, she yelled, "Anyone up there?"

She heard a rattle and then the sound of something like a bowling ball being rolled across the floor above her. A chill ran up the back of her neck, and she shivered.

Merrilee started to back away from the stairs as she saw a paint can hit the wall opposite the upstairs landing and then ricochet towards the steps. It rebounded down hitting first one step and then the next. On the fifth step, the top flew off and blue paint spewed everywhere.

With her back still to the front door, Merrilee reached for her handbag on the side table and stumbled across the threshold into the fresh air outside.

*****

Merrilee couldn't remember exactly what she'd told the waitress when, after leaving the house that day, she tried to steady her nerves over a cup of coffee at the local café in town. Or perhaps she'd talked too much to the desk clerk when she checked into the Hampton Inn unable to say exactly how long she'd be there. He'd commented on all the work she was having done on that old plantation home and asked her if they'd run her out with the noise. Whatever she had revealed, rumors abounded within hours.

The relatives called countless times and cousins offered one suggestion after another. Overnight her house had become the favorite family dinner conversation.

"Perhaps Merrilee was just exhausted. After all she'd had become rather fanatical about the whole renovation thing, and one's imagination could run amuck with fatigue."

"There are priests who deal with exorcisms. Maybe she should contact one of them?"

"Smudging with white sage that you've lit to create smoke in every room will do it. Perhaps a circle of sea salt around the house if that didn't work." Two sisters offered to come over during the next full moon to help out.

And then Sarah Beth, the cousin with the chemistry degree from Clemson, phoned. "Listen," she said. "Have you checked for a gas leak? You may have a gas leak in the house that causes hallucinations. And what about that painter? You even said you thought he'd been drinking."

But Merrilee ignored them all.

A "For Sale" sign went up the next day.

Summer Sounds

Barbara Covington

Mamma's feet pushed because my feet couldn't. The swing went back and forth, and the cool evening air rushed by us. I heard the crickets singing, whippoorwills calling, and children getting a few more minutes of playtime before dark. A buzzing screech caught my attention as a night hawk dove to catch an insect.

But the saddest sound was the shivering owl in the big pine tree by the garden. People said that sound meant someone was dying. I learned later this wasn't true because someone dies somewhere every second, and there are not enough owls on earth to signal that. But a youngster can believe in almost anything.

I loved swinging with Mamma in the summer evenings in our homemade swing that Daddy hung for us, and I loved listening to all the late evening sounds. It was a peaceful time after all the work on the farm stopped for the day.

As I sat listening to the squeak, squeak, of the swing, I noticed smoke from the chimneys of the sharecropper houses, drifting across the grey-orange evening sky. Supper was cooking.

Sometimes we swung as we waited for the mailman. One such evening he delivered a package too large for the mailbox. His horn blared, and we went to meet the car. The mailman reached around to the back seat and lifted a large flat box. That particular box made sounds I recognized as the peeps of little biddies. But I was surprised the baby chickens arrived by mail.

A foul, musty odor rose up to us when Mama opened the box. Three little biddies lay unmoving, not making a sound. They looked as if they had been stepped on as others tried to get out of the box. I buried them in my gold fish grave yard.

The house for the biddies was like a large cage. The chicken house, for older chickens, was bigger and had tobacco sticks attached across from side to side on which the chickens roosted at night. I always wondered if they fell off when they slept. The house itself was low enough for my sister and me to crawl on top with help from a block of wood. This was a special place to play and sleep on hot nights. All we needed was one of Mama's quilts for our bed, and we were set to enjoy gazing at the stars, listening to the frogs in the near-by pond, and to the loud sound of cicadas.

I loved all the sounds, but my favorite came around once a week as Mama and I sat in the swing. I would grab Mamma's arm and say, "Did you hear that?"

She would pat my leg and say, "Yes honey, it's coming."

The horn blew about every five or ten minutes, sometimes longer, as it drew closer and closer to our house. My excitement grew with every sound that was louder knowing it was getting closer, and I would ready myself to jump down from the swing to run to the road. Finally, the horn blasted loudest and strongest one more time, and I knew 'The Rolling Store' had arrived.

The Rolling Store was actually a big van truck converted into a store that carried all kinds of essentials and goodies. It stopped at each house where someone waited by the road. I didn't go to a real store very often, so the Rolling Store was a treat.

Mama and I waited on the side of the road as the truck stopped. The driver let down a tail gate, and we climbed inside. The smell of ripe bananas hit me first thing. They hung in a bunch on one side of the truck where shelves were slanted backwards so nothing would slide out while the truck moved.

On the other side was a counter that held many eatables; among them was a round, wooden box of cheese and a long roll of bologna.

Mama always bought two items for herself; a cinnamon bun covered with smooth white icing and a big wedge of cheese cut from the cheese in the box. She bought me chocolate, vanilla, and strawberry BB Bats and some squirrel Nuts, Mary Janes, and little wax bottles about three inches tall filled with brightly-colored sugar water.

We would take our goodies back to the swing to sit, eat, and continue listening to the night sounds including the sound of The Rolling Store winding up the dirt road where others like us waited impatiently.

Soon the afternoon passed into evening, and Mama and I watched the golden sunset across the fields and again welcomed the night time sounds of rural South Carolina.

*This essay was printed in part in *She Magazine* July 2015.

Swamp Biscuits

Jean Bell

Shortly after the bloodhounds in the swamp picked up the scent of the escapees, kitchen staff delivered a tray of ham biscuits to the prison lobby. Then inmate workers wheeled in a big coffee urn and plugged it in, right in front of the barred, bullet-proof glass of the small Control Room.

While the coffee perked, several officers in the Control Room juggled phones and walkie-talkies, speaking in the urgency of '10-code,' the nationally standardized shorthand for law enforcement. The only phrase I understood were the brusque '10-4's' I learned from the movies. While the officers worked, they stepped around the stack of shotguns leaning against the bars, ready to be issued.

This escape happened the second month of my new job at the prison farm, located in the middle of 7,000 acres of swampland, wetlands, and farmland. Significant differences already contrasted this counseling job with my former one in downtown Baltimore. But even give the differences, I felt surprised that a prison escape prompted a party. Even on my Zen, easy-breathing terms, a celebration before the apprehension of the inmates seemed a little excessive.

Nevertheless, the dew-drop glisten of grease sparkling on the ham slices definitely called my name. My greasy new friend said, "Hello, you sweet girl. We do ham good here in South Carolina. And you don't have to worry about that nasty sauerkraut they serve it with up North."

Accepting the spread before me as another example of Southern hospitality, I reached my hand toward a biscuit.

Just then, a real voice spoke to me with the sweet, steel-like tones of the Warden's secretary. "Bless your heart. Don't those look just good enough to eat?" Her syrupy smile interrupted me mid-reach with the same effect as a slap across my knuckles. "I'm sure the stakeout officers will leave behind nothing but crumbs," she said.

I busied my wayward fingers by straightening napkins on the table that needed no straightening. My cheeks flushed; my eyes blinked; my hand felt numb and clumsy.

"Yes, they sure do look good. It's such a nice treat for the search crew," I said. Since I had been in Carolina only a short time, I didn't know to add the obligatory 'Ma'am' to my pleasantry. But I had a quick teacher, as she showed me by example.

"Oh yes, Ma'am, we do want to feed our men."

Here she paused, to be certain I caught her correction, as she reached to re-straighten the napkins messed up by my earlier straightening. "But of course we don't think of it as just a 'treat'. It's the only hot meal break the escape crew will have until those convicts get caught."

We stood near each other, merged in our awkward pretend pleasantness. If she'd said 'scoundrels' instead of 'convicts,' I would have sworn we bonded together in a time-travel blend of a "Gunsmoke" episode filmed in Mayberry. Naturally, I wanted to be the sexy Miss Kitty of Dodge City looking down my abundant cleavage at her little Aunt Bee.

As years went by and my counseling job merged with the security side of the incarceration business, the peculiarities of food in prison life presented itself time and again. I came to understand that food stood for more than sustenance.

One particular event served up that ham biscuit memory as years later, I made my way through the twilight noises of the swamp, down the dirt roads on the prison property, to deliver food to officers on a stakeout.

Shallow ditches lined the road. Heavy brush and tangled vines blocked my view past a few yards. Getting closer to the post, I cut off the walkie-talkie in my lap, losing the comfort of my colleagues' voices as they reported their positions to the Control Room. With the loss of their presence, I moved the shotgun closer to the comfort of my knee. The radio silence close to the stake-out made it harder for the escapee to spot the officer. Of course, if an inmate did hide nearby, he would see the officer approach my vehicle. But this sergeant had served many stake-out duties over the years, so he moved quickly and quietly to the car's open window.

"Thanks, Ma'am," he muttered as I handed two packages to him. The first package held egg biscuit sandwiches and several apples. The second bag had a tall container of hot coffee. He stuffed the food packages under his poncho, juggling his own shotgun.

"You're welcome," I whispered. Aware of the comfort of my car and his exposure to the mosquitoes and no-see-ums circling around, I slipped him my can of bug spray. "Here's some more spray, in case you run out." He nodded, and I nodded, and before I straightened the car back to the road, he disappeared into the noisy mist, headed back to the shelter of a large oak tree, under a kudzu umbrella that camouflaged him from sight.

As I drove off, I regretted that the ham sandwiches of previous years no longer fit on the menu. My job as an administrator taught me new worries. I gained respect for the

Warden's secretary from years before. Even then, she had guarded resources for those who needed them most.

Our protein menu narrowed primarily to eggs and cheese due to prison budget cuts. The poultry house on prison property provided all of our eggs, as well as teaching inmates the poultry business. The cheese used in the cafeteria came from the "gubment," as the older inmates liked to say. Clearly the cheese had not been born as a good Gouda churned by calloused hands in a cold Wisconsin dairy and sent with best wishes down to this Carolina prison farm. No, this cheese had a kind of, sort of, pedigree, close enough to meet the nutritional standards of the "gubment."

As one inmate joked, "Think of this cheese as processed polyester, and you won't be disappointed." He laughed at his own joke and added, "I didn't do so well as a car thief, but I'm a hell of a food critic."

Ironically, our prison cafeteria arrived early to the "farm to table" trend of fancy cafes. In addition to eggs, we also had a dairy, a hog nursery, and a large vegetable garden. Our inmates enjoyed ready access to healthy, fresh food. Much of the products sold quickly to outside vendors, and even more shipped out to other prisons in the state. For all of our state prisons, nutritionists in headquarters juggled budget limitations with the mandatory dietary requirements.

Even though many prisoners thrived on junk food during their life on the street, once incarcerated, they became savvy consumers, ever mindful of the requirements of the statewide menus. Ever conscious of their legal rights to proper nutrition, these nutritional requirements made common sense because inmates had no freedom to run to Walgreen's for constipation or heartburn problems brought on by inadequate prison food.

This issue of food requirements as legal rights carried particular weight when emergencies required inmates to be restricted to their cells without access to school or the cafeteria. For such occasions, a special menu of 'lock-up' bags came available, to be delivered to all the cells. This process continued for every meal until the institution declared a return to normal movement.

But in the meantime, the bag menu requirements even specified the number of carrot strips needed to accompany an inmate's peanut butter sandwich. If in the monotony of preparing the bags, a carrot strip got omitted, an inmate had a right to sue for denying him food. This meant that a bored inmate could imagine a long list of bounty from his lawsuit. In reality, such a suit would be thrown out by the court. But in the meantime, a guy could dream.

Once during a lockdown from a gang disturbance, an inmate called his attorney to complain about his sour carton of milk. The attorney called the Control Room to ask how the inmate could call given no access to the public phones due to the lockdown. The shake-down team searched the inmate's cell and found a contraband cell phone hidden in the trash, carefully buried under his carrots and milk carton.

Not only did the inmate get food requirements that day, but he certainly received due justice although not quite the justice he had in mind when he made the prohibited call.

One of the trickiest issues dealing with food in prison occurred with the need to balance safety with the charity of community groups. Central to the traditions of worship groups, the value of food could not be over-stated. Just as in neighborhood services, so, too, did volunteers want to bring treats along with their prison ministry.

As a Southern joke goes, when two or more Baptists are gathered in His name, a chicken must die; when two or more Presbyterians gather, there is a casserole in their midst. In this same spirit, most volunteer groups wished to bring something to 'sweeten the process' of gathering in the chapel. They wanted to bring with them 'a little somethin-somethin.'

When I first heard that southern phrase 'somethin-somethin,' I assumed the older church leader had memory problems and couldn't quite recall the specific treat on their menu. "Excuse me, sir. I'm not sure what you said. What did your group want to bring in?" I used my most polite voice.

"Just a little somethin'-somethin.' Not too much," he answered.

"Excuse me again, but not too much of what?"

After a few rounds of this, I grew certain he had a touch of dementia, and he most likely thought I had a whole lot of hearing loss, we decided that it would be fine for his group to bring in some cookies.

For prison officials, no clarity existed for deciding which inmates carried sincere hearts for their use of the chapel for prayer and which inmates carried sincerity for access to the donated cakes, fruit, and pies. Staff did know for certain, though, that any recipe containing sugar carried a guaranteed source for making prison alcohol known as buck.

Any alcohol, even that blessed by its origination in the chapel, guaranteed problems. All a recipe for buck needed— sugar and yeast—could be found in a simple cinnamon bun. If the mixture nestled long enough around a simple heat source, such as a motor in an air conditioner unit, it produced buck. Add some citrus such as an orange from another volunteer event, and eventually, Dom Perignon bubbled forth.

The primary goal of a prison official was for everyone to make it home safely. This goal includes volunteers, staff, and inmates, regardless whether the time frame falls within an hour, a shift, or a thirty year prison sentence. And the emotions of prison—anger, sadness, and greed—when stoked by buck, guaranteed a fight and injuries, which definitely hinders accomplishing that goal.

As the decades passed in my employment, the days of glistening grease on cola-soaked hams became much harder to find in southern prisons. Budget restraints, religious constraints, and health concerns accelerated the rarity of pork on the menu. But some preferences did not fade.

Shortly before my retirement, I joined a group of night shift officers in the cafeteria. One aging geezer, well, yes, we *were* about the same age, reminisced about his best breakfast on the job. He remembered a morning, years before, eating an egg sandwich underneath a kudzu drape while on stake-out duty.

A second officer with us complained about the complexity of the new dietary regulations, then sipped her coffee and said, "As long as I have a little coffee and a whole lot of Jesus, I am good with the world."

But then another guy, much younger, made his second trip through the cafeteria line. When he got back to our table, his mouth full of food and a pile of "gubment" cheese on his plate, he mumbled, "I tell you what, there's nothing better than some good ole prison grits."

Hmmm, seems like someone wrote a book about prison grits.

Joe's Hole

Sammy Rhodes

I don't think I could have been much more than four or five years old when I first visited Joe's Hole, and it was just what the name says it was—a hole in the dirt. But Joe's Hole, in particular, lay in a cleared out space at the end of a quarter mile dirt road surrounded by the Scape Ore swamp, and it was filled with deep, black water.

The Scape Ore stream and its swamp begin with water running down a few hills between Bishopville and Kershaw. It continues southward through Manville, on between Oswego and St. Charles, and brushes the back side of Mayesville before feeding into Rocky Bluff Swamp near Concord.

Joe's Hole was located in the Mayesville community. The dirt road entrance was off of the old part of the Sumter road that ran behind Willy Mayes' store and Sleepy Tisdale's house before intersecting with the new Sumter road, Highway 76.

How long Joe's Hole had been there before my first visit, I am not sure. I am just as unsure as to who and when anyone might have last visited there. All I am sure of is that it existed and seemed to have been a place of fun, relaxation, comfort, and perhaps a safe haven for Mayesville's male members of America's Greatest Generation, the veterans of World War II. Those same members went by nicknames, as unique and unusual as the men themselves. Names like: Blackie, Muddy, Skunk, Goosefoot, Slim, Cuz, Red, Spoony, Unc, Bubba Jim, Edibo, Pot, who was my Uncle Bill and who at that time lived in Charlotte, and, of course, my daddy, 'Bride.

I do not remember any fear and trepidation on my part as I rode with Daddy in his '53 green pickup to Joe's Hole on that initial visit. For all I knew, we were going to Sumter to pick up some steaks from Dewey the butcher or to get a haircut from Marvin or Bill at the barbershop. Although I do remember thinking that we usually did those things on Saturday morning, and that particular day was not Saturday.

Not until Daddy turned his pickup onto that dirt road and asked if I was up for a little swim, did I begin to experience a little nervousness. *We had no swimming trunks.*

I had been to the beach on vacation a couple of times and had been swimming some at the Elk's Club pool in Sumter with my Aunt Frances, so it registered with me that swimming trunks were a natural part of swimming.

Yet, there we were with Daddy asking if I wanted to swim knowing full well we had no swimming trunks. But then I relaxed thinking maybe this place provided trunks and towels.

No sooner had I convinced myself that that was surely the deal, the dirt road opened into a cleared out spot where several vehicles were parked along the edges of the swamp. Up ahead, I could hear laughter and the sound of people splashing in the water somewhere off to my right.

"Okay, sport," Daddy said, shutting off the engine. "Take your clothes off here and leave 'em in the truck."

I remember looking at him and asking, "But where are my trunks?"

"You don't need them here," Daddy replied. He ignored the look of confusion on my face and opened the truck door, got out and began stripping off his own clothes. Totally unsure, I did the same—only I remained inside the pickup to do it. I suppose somewhere in the back of my mind I believed he'd surely surprise me with some trunks—from somewhere. But no such luck.

"Come on, boy," Daddy commanded.

Even more nervous, I slid out of the truck and fell in behind him to walk toward the other four or five men. Sure enough, they were standing there without bathing suits, too. I then noticed there were three or four other boys there, naked as well. The men were Edibo, Muddy, Billy, Red, and Harvey,

Jr. The boys were Bill, Red, Jr., Skip, and Michael. Bill was a couple of years older than me and already a Boy Scout. The others were a couple of years younger.

We neared the group. "Hey, Bride," Muddy yelled out to Daddy, "We got a cold stream running today. You and Sammy come on and cool off."

The men and boys stood naked on two slabs of concrete, each slab about 8ft. by 8ft. and melded together by an exposed iron tie rod. And like any time when you get a group of boys or men together, there is always a certain amount of pecker-checking-out going on. A four or five year old has an eye level view with these strange appendages sort of flopping around in front of you. Everyone did their appropriate amount of checking, and then Daddy grabbed me by the hand and drug me with him from the concrete slabs into what I was sure was my death—the deep, dark water of Scape Ore Swamp. I hid my fear well by not crying out.

The swimming hole was an open area of water on the edge of the swamp about the size of two backyard pools put together. Nowhere in that entire area could the boys or the men stand with their heads above water, so Daddy put his right arm around me and dog paddled around the area to give me a feel for the hole. While I floated under his pull, I could hear Red and Edibo talking.

"Hey Red," Edibo yelled. "Did I tell you 'bout those two water moccasins I killed out here last week? They were sunnin' up there on the slabs."

"No, you didn't," Red replied, but I seen a couple of alligators earlier this morning in this water here."

This conversation was certainly of no comfort to me at all. In my mind, every leaf or twig I touched below the water's surface was a moccasin striking my naked little pecker making it swell up twice the size of me, or an alligator or turtle biting it completely off.

When Daddy and I made our way around the pool and back to the slabs, I finally felt safe again. The other boys jumped in and climbed out of the water on their own. But I stayed put. I thought they were idiots.

"You want to join the other boys, son?" Daddy asked.

Looking back over the surface of the dark water and thinking of what might lay beneath it, I didn't hesitate in my answer. "No, sir. I don't feel so good. My appendix is hurting."

How I knew anything about appendicitis at my tender age is beyond me, but that's what I told him. It worked. He took me back home to Mama, and never in my life had I been so glad to see her.

I did go back to the hole with Daddy six or seven times that summer. I also swam with the other boys and allowed myself to have some fun, but I never once went swimming in

Joe's Hole without feeling I put myself, or at least my penis, in grave danger.

Thinking of it now, I am pretty certain that summer was the last summer any of us used Joe's Hole. Some say it was because Mayesville built a swimming pool behind the Presbyterian Church that ended its run. Others say it was because the men became too embarrassed to go back again after Verna Cooper and some other girl came barreling down that dirt lane with camera out, taking pictures of them naked.

I will never know what actually brought about the end of Joe's Hole, but I think about it from time to time in quiet moments of reminiscing. And what I think about most when I think of Joe's Hole is not how it ended, but rather how the hell it came to be in the first place. The beginning puzzles me a lot more than the ending. What made grown men shed their clothes and drag their naked sons down to the middle of a moccasin-snapping turtle- alligator infested hole of swamp water?

Maybe it was just a way of cooling off after steaming days of work in the fields. Maybe it was just a habit born from not wanting to end the day too quickly.

Or maybe it was the simple need to spend time in the company of others, bonding and re-bonding in the pure nakedness of the male world with men who had once fought alongside of each other and with the sons they desperately hoped to protect from having to do the same.

The School Chair Incident

Brian Cope

We don't know how the school chair got lodged into the aluminum johnboat, but it wasn't coming loose, no matter how hard we tried. Morgan kicked it. Richie kicked it. I kicked it. Hard. It didn't budge. Ray stood the 12-foot long boat up on its stern, then pushed it forward. The school chair hit the dirt first, but instead of popping out of the boat, it supported the weight of it as the boat teetered like a see-saw.

Ray flipped the boat upright, sat in the school chair, and nodded in satisfaction. "I'll sit in the school chair," he said.

With that, we launched. Richie and I were in one boat, Morgan and Ray in the other. The backrest on the school chair was actually pretty comfortable, Ray said, and he seemed happy with it.

It wasn't a school desk with a writing surface, but a school chair with shiny metal legs and a hard plastic seat and backrest like what you'd find in a school library. The legs pinched the bench seat of the boat, and the feet were lodged in between two support ribs just perfectly to keep it in place as though designed to offer Ray the best seat in the Rocky Bluff Swamp of Sumter County, a favorite fishing hole of ours.

It was March. A warm day, but the water was still cold as winter reluctantly began to let go its grasp on this part of the world. The cypress trees lining the blackwater swamp were just beginning to bud, sucking just enough water off the stream to make it fishable from our small boats.

Paddling only to avoid downed logs or to navigate the sharp turns, we drifted with the current, tossing small spinning lures with ultralight rods and reels, catching redbreast, the brightly-colored panfish closely related to bluegill. While bluegill are found in every body of water in the Palmetto State, redbreast only live in swampy ecosystems like this.

After catching a few nice fish in one spot, we anchored both boats to fish more thoroughly. But before making another cast, Morgan put his index finger to his lips. The international "quiet" sign. He pointed toward shore where just off the water in the rich, black mud, we spotted a large beaver standing upright, doing its best to hide behind a small sapling that barely covered the animal's face.

A foot or more of the beaver's body protruded from both sides of the tree. But convinced it was out of our sight, it peeked its head around and then quickly pulled it behind the sapling again for fear of us spotting it.

We all chuckled quietly, eased our anchors back into the boats, allowed the current to move us along, and let the beaver think it had gotten one over on us.

A few minutes later, we were catching fish again downstream and finally laughing out loud about the stealthy beaver.

"What's with the water cooler?" Richie asked Morgan, noticing the tall, 5-gallon container that would look more at home on the sidelines of a football field than in a fishing boat. I had meant to ask the same question when launching the boats, but like everyone else at the time, was too flustered about the school chair.

"Watermelon. A big one. On ice," answered Morgan. "And after we eat it, we can put our stringers of fish in there."

"From Minnie B's? In Florida?" I asked.

"You know it. She grows the best. Dad brought it up yesterday," Morgan answered.

"Oh man, that's gonna be some kind of good. The one you brought last year — juiciest ever!" said Richie.

I smiled inside and out, realizing I'd left our sandwiches in the truck, but wouldn't have to face the wrath of hungry friends thanks to Morgan and his watermelon. My stomach was already moaning, and a quarter of a watermelon would be just the ticket.

"Man, I can't thank you enough for bringing that along," I said.

"You know I'm always looking out for the fellas. And besides, this cooler," Morgan said as he slapped a hand on the cooler's top, "could double as a seat."

"Don't need it for a seat when I've got the school chair," said Ray, sitting casually with his legs extended, setting the hook on another fish.

"Hey, look. Another redbreast," he said, leaning slightly toward the water to grab the fish.

And just then, the school chair popped loose.

The noise alerted me just in time to look up and see the expression on Ray's face turn from relaxed to panicked denial. The chair's much delayed reaction from our earlier efforts to dislodge it turned it into an ejection seat.

Ray, still seated in the chair, tried desperately to stay out of the drink cooler and grabbed at anything as both he and the chair made their way over the side. A surprised look of satisfaction momentarily overcame his face as he found the handle to the watermelon cooler, which offered zero support to Ray's effort to stay aboard. Still seated perfectly in the chair, he hit the water, squealed at the wet coldness, and then watched helplessly as the top of the water cooler came loose, bonking him in the face, followed by a cascade of ice. Finally, the watermelon itself punched Ray squarely in the nose.

Richie and I both fell to the floor of our boat, partly from uncontrollable laughter and partly in fear that we'd fall overboard ourselves from laughing so hard.

Morgan mustered up a bit more sympathy, chuckling only slightly before paddling the front of his boat toward Ray, who didn't yet see the humor in the situation. Ray's a pretty funny guy, but he was outdoing himself here. It was a crying shame that he couldn't appreciate it.

The floating cooler bumped up against our boat. Richie grabbed it while I grabbed the lid. Then we all watched the watermelon float downstream out of sight bringing protests from us all.

Believing the fun was over and that it was time to focus on getting Ray warm and dry, I noticed Morgan's chuckling turn to horror as Ray pushed down hard on the side of the boat in a feeble attempt to fling himself aboard. Actually, it was hard to tell if Ray wanted back in the boat, or if he wanted everything inside it to join him in the cold, swampy water, which is exactly what happened.

With no watermelon cooler to reach back for as the boat completely flipped, Morgan instead sort of flung himself toward Ray, as if hoping Ray would catch him before he hit the water. It didn't work out for him, but for Richie and me, it was plenty funny to watch.

Ray stood shivering, both hands to his face, "I think my nose is broken," he said.

Morgan hunched down in the waist deep water, feeling along the bottom for their sunken fishing rods and other equipment, then looked downstream past Richie and me.

"Well, well, welcome to the party," he said through chattering teeth.

Richie and I turned to see our other friend Dalton who had launched his kayak downstream from us that morning. He paddled toward us, looking down into the bay of his kayak.

Dalton finally looked up at the scene, mouth wide open in confusion as his bulging eyes scanned the area. Then he reached down, groaned loudly for effect, and hefted up our lost fruit.

He grinned. "Watermelon, anyone?"

Waiting for Norman Rockwell

(Along a South Carolina Highway)

Gloria Dahl

S pringtime, and a man named Gideon sits on a wooden crate in front of a convenience store. He holds a chipped stoneware cup in one hand, a cigarette in the other. Methodically he takes a sip of coffee and then a drag from his cigarette.

Tall and big-boned, his shoulders curl slightly forward and down causing his suspenders to look too short and as if they have bent his frame. There is an air of meekness about him that seems at odds with his size.

His skin, leathered, makes him appear in his mid-seventies, but a shock of brown hair peeks out from the baseball cap he wears, belying the ravages of the sun. He remains stone-faced until a customer walks by. There is nothing sinister about Gideon, no reason to fear he might jump up from the crate and ask for a handout. But still, the customer does a quick side-step to try to avoid him. Gideon nods, ducks his head, and studies his fingernails.

Behind him loom two plate glass windows plastered with signs:

BEER

FISHING TACKLE

LIVE BAIT

PARKING FOR CUSTOMERS ONLY!

AIR—75¢

WE APPRECIATE YOUR BUSINESS

---NO LOITERING---

Gideon asks nothing of anyone. He just sits and watches the highway, as though he waits for something. Some days he does odd-jobs. Once in a while, someone pays him to cut grass or to help with home repairs.

I do not know his story, where he came from, or whatever addiction, if any, he might have, whether he has family, or even a friend. He never appears to talk at length with anyone at the store. And yet, the times I see him, he speaks to me without saying a word.

Late afternoon, and I study him. Gideon walks the quarter mile to an old cemetery and down a narrow pathway. He disappears into the tree line. Homeless whether or not by choice, he lives and sleeps near the river. His tattered tent is secured to the ground by ropes attached to old railroad pins driven into the ground. A few other journeyers pass through, but he doesn't bother them, and they, likewise. None of them are supposed to be there.

Once before, as I turned onto the road by the cemetery, I thought I'd seen a ghost weaving among the headstones. Then, I realized it was a woman who indeed had become a ghost: A ghost of her former self. And the same could be said of Gideon.

Another daybreak, and I see Gideon heading back into town, back to the crate. The chipped mug, possibly the last relic from his past, dangles from his thumb and forefinger.
He sits. Ponders. Waits and watches for something perhaps even he cannot name.

One day, a faded blue RV pulls off the highway near the river. Crude lettering on the side makes the pronouncement: JESUS SAVES! I envision a traveling preacher, with a sincere and caring heart as he slips and slides down the river bank. Surely there will be some lost soul he can lead to a better way of life, away from the murky waters of hopelessness to the path of Glory. Even if.

Wintertime, and the crate is gone. Gideon is gone. The signs on the windows are gone, torn away by the new owners of the store. And I wonder if what Gideon has waited for has finally arrived.

For me, the storefront has served as a backdrop, the signs and the crates, as props. And in the order of things, Gideon has served as a reflection of the lives of others like him. He was a portrait waiting to be painted and placed within a frame. Waiting to be noticed.

Norman Rockwell never sketched or painted Gideon. But for me, the quiet man is a portrait engraved upon my memory and a voice from another time whispers..."There but for the grace..."

A Tent Meeting

Sherry Fasano

Timid young roots earlier introduced to the fertile soil inched downward, taking hold. Before long, vibrant plants blossomed, demanding more and more attention as days stretched long.

Gnarled branches on fruit trees gradually drooped to the ground working bees into a frenzy as their offerings ripened to an almost unbearable sweetness. And wild grapes, swollen with juice intoxicating and addictive, swagged the woods and lured passers-by on hot afternoons.

Shy, soft spring morphed into hot, steamy summer, requiring dawn until dusk labor, and by summers end the body was exhausted, the soul weary.

By the time green leaves faded to gold, the preacher in our small community church announced the date for the annual week-long revival meeting. His Sunday sermons exhorted the flock to examine their souls and prepare for repentance. And even though the majority of folks in the congregation experienced no prickling of conscience, they prayed fervent prayers for known sinners.

While the men set up a great canvas tent at the edge of the woods with rows of wooden benches and a makeshift altar, women prepared pot-luck suppers. These meals had little to do with luck. Family recipes, packed with pride into big baskets and shared each night before the service, fed the crowd and left plenty of leftovers.

Everybody anticipated Mizz Hanes' chicken-n-dumplings, Elsie Starling's fresh butter beans, and Granny Peake's ten-layer chocolate cake. China platters heaped with fried chicken, biscuits, and crackling cornbread crowded between crocks of freshly churned butter and jars of golden honeycombs.

Following supper, musicians tuned their instruments, strumming together, while children ran and played. Guitars, banjos, and fiddles harmonized in familiar old songs as the crispness of the autumn evening fell. When we gathered and sang,

"There is pow'r, pow'r,
wonder working pow'r
In the blood,
of the Lamb...;"

The spirit always moved, and one of the old folks caught a glimpse of glory. As if by magic, she threw down her cane and ran the aisles shouting, "Hallelujah!" with hands held high and a smile lighting the creases of her wizened face. Children pointed, and their parents nodded and smiled as they sang out loud and clear, tapping their toes in time to the music.

By the time the preacher stepped behind the pulpit, round faced toddlers, heavy lidded and quiet, snuggled into the folds of their mama's soft cotton dresses. The preacher began speaking with laughter in his voice, but when he approached the subject of sin his voice rose. His fists banged the pulpit and drove wide-eyed children close to their mama's shoulders. All those dozing after the hearty supper sat up straight and offered their undivided attention.

The preacher acknowledged sin's shiny allure and warned, "The consequences of disappointment and shame will surely follow. But we all sin," he reminded. "We're born into sin. Is there hope for imperfect people living in an imperfect world? Yes indeed Brother Miles," he shouted as he looked toward the Amen Corner where Brother Miles sat nodding his head with vigor.

"You can count on it. Am I right, Sister Viola?" He pointed to a deacon's wife sitting in the front row.

Cardboard hand fans advertising the funeral home flapped the air in unison as Sister Viola flashed her gapped-toothed smile and waved an embroidered handkerchief in answer.

"You see, my friends, Hope was born of a virgin in the ancient town of Bethlehem almost two thousand years ago. And Hope has a name: Jesus. As the Son of God, and a young Jewish man, Jesus collected twelve disciples and, with those twelve, walked dusty roads, preaching on hillsides and beside the Sea of Galilee.

"He fed the hungry and turned water into wine. With great compassion He healed the sick, raised the dead, and made the blind to see. To all who listened, He explained how to become a child of God. He offered hope to imperfect people living in an imperfect world.

"During this time, Jesus gathered a great many followers. But after several years His popularity scared the Jewish leaders so they plotted His death. Betrayed by one of His own disciples and captured in a garden by Roman soldiers, all of His followers, in fear, denied Jesus and scattered."

Having secured the congregation's full attention, the preacher paused and mopped his brow with his handkerchief before he continued, "The soldiers brought Jesus before the Roman governor, Pontius Pilate, who actually found no fault in Him. But the crowd demanded, 'Crucify! Crucify!' So a reluctant Pilate handed Jesus over to them.

"With a crown of thorns forced upon his head, and His back torn open by a whip, Jesus struggled under the weight of a rough wooden cross up to a hill called Golgotha. There, the Son of God hung on that cross between two thieves.

"While one thief cursed Jesus, the other thief confessed his own sins and acknowledged Jesus as the Son of God. To that imperfect person, Jesus promised eternal life, beginning that very day."

A soft breeze rustled the trees outside of the tent and the preacher lowered his voice,

"Late that afternoon while the crowd mocked and spat, the skies blackened, the wind whipped, and Jesus looked toward the heavens and pleaded, 'Father forgive them, for they know not what they do.' Then Jesus cried, 'It is finished.' And with those last words, He died."

Someone in the congregation sniffed as the preacher continued, "Some of His followers removed His body from the cross and placed it in a borrowed tomb. A large stone sealed the entrance to the tomb and a Roman soldier stood guard there so his body wouldn't be moved. At this point, friends, it appeared all hope was gone. But wait, I'm not finished."

Several men standing near the back of the tent called out, "Preach on," and raised their hands. The preacher nodded and resumed, "Early in the morning, on the third day, two women who had been followers of Jesus walked to the tomb carrying spices to prepare His body for burial. When they got to the tomb, do you know what they found? Do you know, Brother Ralph?"

Brother Ralph, sitting in the second row by Sister Etta Mae, his wife of over sixty years, called out, "An empty tomb, Preacher."

The preacher nodded and sipped water from a paper cup, then in a hoarse voice continued, "That's right, Brother Ralph. An empty tomb. Hallelujah! Jesus had risen, just as He said He would. Hope was, and still is, very much alive."

Tears glistened in eyes and spilled down cheeks as the preacher, once again, explained acknowledgement of sin, repentance, God's forgiveness, and the sweetness of grace. The musicians softly sang,

"Just as I am, without one plea,

But that Thy blood was shed for me,

And that Thou bidst me come to Thee,

Oh Lamb of God, I come!

I come!"

And come they did. By the dim, flickering light of lanterns folks made their way to the makeshift altar. Those who had earlier examined their souls and found no sin, knelt shoulder to shoulder with known sinners.

There at the edge of the woods, under an autumn sky filled with stars, tears wet the rough sawn wood as heads bowed, and hearts were made clean.

* * * * *

The cool days of autumn passed and the soil rested, long cleared of the withered brown vines from summer's end. Red birds flitted from tree to tree searching for seeds. A cold wind blew and tiny snowflakes drifted down. Each one different. Intricate. Complete.

Before long, everything was covered in a pure white blanket. Made perfect. Redeemed.

About the Contributors

Dale Barwick is a graduate of Clemson University and now owns Summerton Primary Care where she practices medicine as a Nurse Practitioner.

She has published in medical journals and in *His Mother! Women Write about Their Mothers-in-Law with Humor, Frustration, and Love* and is currently working on two novels.

John Beckham was born in Greer, South Carolina, but moved two hours later to Charleston (actually 4 years, later). He has worked in sales for over 20 years.

The Beckhams have been in SC since pre-Revolutionary War. In fact, John's father wrote five books about growing up in SC. John, himself, golfs a lot, enjoys bourbon, loves all things SC, and hate all things Ohio (maybe not hate). He is also a big fan of UGA.

He is currently at work on a couple books.

Margaret Jean Bell worked for forty years in multiple prisons, several psych hospitals, and one heroin clinic before finally retired. She now writes full time drawing on her experiences and interest in personal dynamics. She is published in *His Mother! Women Write about Their Mothers-in-Law* and is an award-winning author for her essays. Her first novel, *Prison Grits,* was published in 2015, and she is presently at work on her second novel, *Prison Haze.*

L. Thomas-Cook, originally from upstate New York, along with her husband and their best friend, a shorkie named Sonny, moved to the Murrells Inlet community a few years ago. It didn't take long after moving south for the area's history and setting to reignite a desire to be a writer and photographer.

Added inspiration was to serve as a former board member for the South Carolina Writers Association (formerly Writers Workshop) and the 2014 conference chairperson. That experience motivated the start of the Writers and Authors Assistance Group (WAAG), a group of equally dedicated authors who critique, support, and help writers further develop their craft.

"I have an interest in the paranormal and history. Creating stories based on true events is also a passion for my work. I especially love to write about strong characters dealing with inner conflict, and to develop plots with lots of twists and turns. As long as I can do that and toss in a bit of humor, I'm happy."

Published works include *In Your Eyes,* a series about undercover detectives living an alternate lifestyle during the 1980's in Florida. Volume 1 is available on Kindle and Amazon. Coming soon in spring 2018 is a novel published by Deer Hawk Publishing entitled *Forgiveness,* a supernatural, murder suspense.

Brian Cope has a B.A. in English Literature with a concentration in writing from the University of South Carolina. He's a fishing columnist and feature writer for *Carolina Sportsman Magazine* and the editor of *CarolinaSportsman.com*. He's a proud native of wonderful, wild 'n wacky South Cackalacky.

Barbara Covington was born and raised in rural South Carolina, but lived in several other states before returning to her home town in Florence, South Carolina, to enjoy her "golden years." She thinks there is nowhere better to live and enjoys writing of her wonderful experiences of living in South Carolina.

Her two religious published books, *Peter's Walk With Jesus* and *Mary's Ponderings*, can be found on Amazon. Barbara states that as she was studying and feeling what they must have felt, she found herself actually feeling their feelings more and more. "I became immersed in their lives to the extent I felt their pain and joy."

Ryan Crawford was born in Honea Path, SC, and attended Clemson University before joining the Peace Corps. While traveling with his wife, he published poetry and fiction in *New York Quarterly*, *Torpedo*, *Borderlands*, *Anon*, and other journals. He has an MFA from Southern Illinois University where he is currently a Ph.D. student studying the neuroscience of insight in the rhetoric and composition program.

Gloria Dahl is a multi-genre writer and musician who began her writing career in the greeting card field. Since then, she has written and published dozens of human interest features about people and places in South Carolina.

Gloria is also a poet. Some of her earlier writings can be seen at wordpress.com.

She is working on a book titled, *In My Mother's Shadow*.

What she loves best is family, sweet tea, homemade ice cream, and bluegrass music.

Gloria lives in Upstate South Carolina.

Sherry Fasano lives in a small town in South Carolina with her husband and their hound dog, Lizzie. Her favorite hobbies include porch sitting and spinning tall tales for her grandchildren, often enjoyed simultaneously. She's been writing family stories and fiction for several years.

Her short story, "The Gift of Understanding," was published in the anthology, *The Old Weird South* (QW Publishers 2013).

Martha Dabbs Greenway is a seventh generation South Carolinian and lives at Dabbs Crossroads in a rambling country farm house built by her grandaddy. Co-founder of Southern Sampler Artists' Colony and retired Director of the Sumter County Cultural Commission, Martha lives contentedly with her two cats: Sonoma, rescued on the Northern California coast, and Salem, an orange tabby who showed up on her porch while Martha was reading a book about an orange cat dropped at a library in Iowa.

Her work is published in *A Southern Sampler*, *Charleston and The South*, *Serving Up Memory* and *What I Wish I Could Tell You*.

Johnny Hilton is a graduate of the University of South Carolina where he earned a B.A. in Political Science, an M.ED.in Secondary Social Studies, and a Ph.D. in Education Administration. He lives in Sumter, South Carolina where he served as a teacher and principal in the public schools of Sumter for 35 years and is currently a member of the Sumter School District Board of Trustees.

His family includes his son John, an attorney and real estate entrepreneur, daughter-in-law Page, an attorney, daughter Margaret, a graduate student studying to become a psychologist, and Daisy, a rescued Golden Retriever.

Johnny loves making music, writing songs, and spending time with family and friends. He also enjoys being outdoors, writing stories, interacting with young people, and swimming. He can be contacted at www.johnnyhilton.com www.johnbhiltonjr.blogspot.com and www.thefootnotes.com

Kathryn Etters Lovatt earned her M.A. in Creative Writing and English from Hollins University. She continued her studies at Hong Kong University, where she taught American Studies.

A former winner of the Doris Betts Prize, Kathryn also won *Press 53*'s short story prize. A Virginia Center of the Arts Fellow, her work has most recently appeared in *North Carolina Literary Review* on line and m*oonShine Review* as well as in the anthologies *Serving Up Memory*, *What I Wish I could Tell You* and *His Mother*.

Kathryn received a SC Arts Commission individual artist grant for prose in 2013. She lives and writes in Camden, South Carolina.

David Fairley McInnis, Sr. was born in Timmonsville, SC and attended schools there as well as in Sumter, SC. After graduating from Edmunds High School in Sumter, he attended the University of North Carolina on a partial diving scholarship. While there, David became the Atlantic Coast Conference diving champion two years in a row. As a tribute to him, UNC now awards the David F. McInnis Award to both male and female diving champions.

After serving in both the Air Force and Air Force Reserves, achieving the rank of Captain, David entered law school at the University of South Carolina while working three jobs: he served as the Assistant Manager of the Sumter Chamber of Commerce and as the manager of the Chambers in both Conway and Lancaster. He also coached the diving team during this time. He graduated law school in 1964, went into private practice for a few years, and later became City Judge for the City of Sumter in 1966.

In 1975, David was elected to the South Carolina State Legislature and served on the Ways and Means Committee and as Chairman of the Rules Committee and Joint Appropriations Review Committee. David became a circuit court judge in 1985 and retired happily in 1995.

He is a recipient of the Order of the Palmetto and a charter inductee in the Sumter Athletic Hall of Fame. But in his words the best thing that ever happened to him occurred in 1958 when he married his "forever" sweetheart, the late Barbara Lee Bruce. Together they have three children, four grandchildren, and three greatgrandchildren.

Susan Doherty Osteen is an Honors Graduate of Journalism from TCU in Fort Worth, Texas, She has worked for a variety of newspapers and non-profit organizations.

In 2010 after more than a decade of collaborative research, she published *Tracing a Legacy*, a 950 page tomb chronicling her family's ranching empire from County Donegal, Ireland, to the American Wild West. Her essay about her mother-in-law is published in *His Mother.*

Susan lives in South Carolina with her husband and two children. She continues to write for regional publications and is working on a three-part novel, as well as attending graduate school at USC Columbia in the MFA program.

Brenda Remmes is the author of the bestselling novel *The Quaker Café* and two other Quaker Café novels titled *Home to Cedar Branch* and her most recent release, *Mama Sadie*. Her stories and articles have appeared in *Newsweek* as well as southern publications and journals.

She currently lives with her husband in an old family home near the Black River Swamp in South Carolina.

Annette Reynolds is a mother of one son now 50, grandmother of eight, two of which are bonus grands, and great-grandmother of six. She is both a divorcee and a widow.

Annette graduated Limestone College with a B.S. degree in Home Economics back when it was called that. She is a member of the Baha'i Faith, the second largest religious tradition in South Carolina. She published the book *Trudy and the Baha'is Spiritual Path in South Carolina.*

She retired from the Clemson University Extension Service after 30 years. She began her career in Colleton County as a 4-H agent and then transferred to Orangeburg County where she received a Master's of Ed. at S.C. State University. After 24 years in Orangeburg County, she finished her career as a Cluster Director in Beaufort, Colleton, and Jasper Counties.

A survivor of domestic violence, Annette calls herself a thriver and published a book about the Battered Women's Movement titled *Survivors Thrive.* She started volunteer work with abused women shortly after arriving in Orangeburg County and continues that work today.

In addition, Annette serves on the Pee Dee Coalition Shelter Advisory Council and as Vice President is liaison to the Pee Dee Coalition's Florence Chapter Board. She is also a contributor to the "Faith and Values" section of the *Florence Morning News.*

Sam Rhodes was born and raised in Mayesville, S.C. He attended Clemson University and then USC where he graduated with a major in History and a minor in English. He later returned to the USC Graduate School of History, but eventually chose joining his Dad in the family's cotton farming operation where he remained for almost twenty years until 1994.

Moving to Greenville, SC, Sam began a sixteen-year career in printing and publishing, and then spent seven years teaching English and History at Horizons School in Atlanta, GA.

Sam's collection of poems *I Saw You Sitting on the Moon* was published in 1997. His essays and articles have also appeared in *The Greenville Journal*, *Greenville Magazine*, *Pee Dee Magazine*, as well as a series of essays entitled "The Color of Testosterone" in *Wake Magazine*. More of his poems were also published in *Wake*.

He is the proud father of four children: Samuel McBride Rhodes II, Elizabeth Caroline Rhodes, Skylar Sumter Rhodes, and Savannah DeLage Rhodes. As the custodial parent of his two youngest daughters, Sam raised Skylar and Savannah to mature young ladies.

He is now the owner of a Signarama franchise.

Sandy Richardson is an Honors Graduate from USC Columbia where she majored in Creative Writing and English. Her first novel, *The Girl Who Ate Chicken Feet,* was published by Dial Books for Young Readers (1998) and received a nomination for the South Carolina Junior Book Award and a listing on Bank Street College's Best Children's Books 1998.

Her other works have appeared in several magazines and anthologies. Her nonfiction piece, "Nana's Basket" was published in *The Pettigru Review* and received a Pushcart Nomination. Sandy also compiled and edited an anthology *His Mother! Women Write about Their Mothers-in-law with Humor, Frustration, and Love,* published by Southern Sass Publishing Alliances (2016), where she serves as editor-in-chief. *His Mother* was a finalist in the nonfiction anthology category for American BookFest Awards for Best Books of 2017. For more information visit: www.SouthernSassPublishingAlliances.com

Sandy is a South Carolinian through and through and never wants to leave. She lives with her husband and two obnoxiously spoiled cats at the edge of a pond filled with bream, bass, geese, and an occasional alligator. The couple has two grown children, a much-loved daughter-in-law, and two cats.

Favorite Writing Advice: "The bigger the issue, the smaller you write....You don't write about the horrors of war. No. You write about a kid's burnt socks lying on the road. You pick the smallest manageable part of the big thing, and you work off the resonance." From Reynolds Price.

Pat Willer is a third generation Kansan. Her work in international education took her to the University of South Carolina in Columbia where she and her husband lived for twenty four years. She loved her family, friends, and work in the South. But upon retirement, she headed back to Lawrence, Kansas to be closer to home.

She is passionate about family, her two grandsons, Beckett and Addy, a golden Doodle named Mac, and politics. Back home in Kansas, she has begun a new career in politics and currently serves as secretary of the Douglas County Democrats. When not working on an impossible mission to turn Kansas blue, she continues to write fiction and hopes to complete a mystery novel.

Jay Wright is a past president of Foothills Writers Guild and currently coordinates publicity and guild publications. He is also husband to Anne, dad to Jim and Jana, and Papa Jay to Addison and Alexa.

Jay is a Vietnam Era vet who hates war, violence, law breaking, law breakers, and freeloaders. On the other hand, he loves writers, writing, travel, old bridges, old churches, old barns, old guitars, guns, flags, confederate battlefields, old graveyards, old statues, coastal photography; & an occasional mug of *Blue Moon* with a big slice of orange.

He is the author of three books and also writes freelance for *Anderson Magazine* and *Fair-Town Times*. His self-published books include: *Appalachian Tales & Stretched Truths* (co-authored with Jim Broome), *Where'd the Sun Go?* (a children's book), and *G.A.S. - Living with Guitar Acquisition Syndrome* (humor for guitar addicts).

Jay considers 2017 the greatest year of his life in spite of worrying about fake news and the adequacy of the world's coffee supply.

A Little Somethin' Extra

A Survey

Sandy Richardson

Out of curiosity and just plain nosiness, I sent out a questionnaire to approximately 100 friends and acquaintances across the state to find out what they like and dislike about living in South Cackalacky. The results are below:

*Every person highly recommended South Carolina as a great place to live. The reasons why included the following: "it's a great place to raise a family; the people are the friendliest of anywhere; taxes are low [although some others might disagree with this notion]; and different types of landscapes can be found here such as: the beautiful coastal area, the piedmont and plains, and the rolling hills and mountains—all within a day's drive from anywhere in the state.

Several mentioned the fresh seafood as high motivation to live here. Three natives wrote, "Don't tell anyone to move here. Keep us a secret!"

And finally, one responder declared: "If you want to experience the best of the South, come to South Carolina. We've never lost our manners, and a few genteel spirits still walk around."

*Favorite spots to visit overwhelmingly include the coast and the mountains, but there were shout-outs also to Greenville, Spartanburg, Columbia, Charleston, and many of the smaller towns like Rockville, Irmo, Camden, and Beaufort. Also popular are Sullivan's Island and the Isle of Palms (especially for the fried oysters at Shem Creek Bar and Grill).

But remarkably, over 75% of the responders replied their favorite spot to visit was home— the small towns, fields, and farms of their childhoods.

*That sentiment spilled over into the question asking for a favorite childhood memory of growing up in South Carolina. Here are some quotes about favorite memories, "the smell of tobacco curing in a hot warehouse," "the cotton fields of Lee County," "the smell of cotton defoliant in September and October mixed with the chill nights of the fall," "Sunday dinner at Grandmamma's house," "walking through our peach orchard with my dog," and "everyday life in my small, rural town."

*Other memories of childhood and teen years centered around trips to the beach and the magic of Myrtle Beach Pavilion with its Boardwalk Ride (both now gone). Some remembered picnics at Poinsett State Park outside of Pinewood and family reunions at Red Bluff in Marlboro County. Many, huge, family reunions were held at state parks across the state where fried chicken, biscuits, and an exceptional number of other side dishes were (and still are) served.

Spring Break weeks at the beach can't be forgotten and include memories of shagging at the OD pavilion and raising a little "Cain" at quiet, sedate, Pawley's Island where the marsh tides rose and ebbed quietly during high school and college years.

Transplants to the state had other equally vivid memories of their times here, most included vacations at the adored beaches or in the mountains. Another respondent wrote that one of her special memories is the Shandon neighborhood in Columbia where she lived for a while before returning to her home state: "the tree-lined streets, tidy brick cottages…so much character…and the unbelievable beauty in the spring when dogwoods and azaleas bloomed."

*Speaking of favorite foods to be found in our state, look for the best barbeque ANYWHERE, EVER. And it should be so because it was in South Cackalacky over five centuries ago that barbeque was born. Today, there are over 250 BBQ restaurants in the state. We have sauces ranging from a vinegar base to a mustard base and others relying on foundations of light tomato or heavy tomato bases.

Other favorite dishes include: shrimp & grits, cheese grits, gravy & grits, and grits just about any way we can fix it.

Fried chicken, red chicken stew (no the chickens are not red), fried shrimp, fried oysters, fried bream, fried crappie—let's face it—most anything fried is good.

Add to that list marinated okra, fried okra, and any number of mouth-watering recipes for mac & cheese. Oh and throw in some cornbread, hushpuppies, or butter biscuits. Also high on the favorite foods of summer is the tomato sandwich (made with Big Boy, Better Boy, Butter Boy, or Early Girl tomatoes), with lots of salt and pepper, all stacked on white bread slathered with Dukes Mayo or Miracle Whip.

Hungry yet?

*Perhaps all those calories are calculated to get you on the dance floor where the shag still reigns as the number one dance in the state. In fact, it is South Carolina's state dance. Most responders stated they loved to Shag. A few denied having any ability at it, and the rest admitted to just fakin' it. And that's okay in South Cackalacky. Most of us are too busy having a good time to pay much attention to your dance steps. It's all about the "feelin'" after all.

*A few of the things that people miss the most from times past are the country juke joints and clubs where Blues and Jazz played all weekend long; small stores in rural areas, low rent, and reasonable coastal real estate prices.

*Of course, there are a few things about present day South Carolina that we lament: we now have to lock our doors at night; littering is at an all-time peak; humidity and mosquitoes seem more relentless than in years gone by, as do the sand fleas and no-see-ums. Then there is the ugly fact that we are often at the top of the list for violent domestic abuse crimes, and tragically, we have failing schools in some areas.

Many of our roads are rough. Traffic can be down-right intimidating in some areas along the coast, especially in tourist season. Locals often grieve the loss of a less crowded space.

A majority of responders red-flagged the deplorable remnants of Jim Crow attitudes still found in the state. Other people mentioned a certain social haughtiness in certain quarters toward outsiders in general. Both situations certainly still exist but, thankfully, whether through good times or heartbreaking events, the problems we have faced and continue to battle are improving and being transformed as South Carolina prospers and grows into itself.

*Much new growth has been seen in the state in terms of attitudes and community activities that bring people together. Responders noted they are loving all the new cuisines sprouting up in restaurants across the state. There's pretty much something for any taste: Indian, Asian, Western, Mexican, Italian, Greek, American, Soul, and Country Cookin'. And farmer's markets and farm to table events have been established throughout the state.

And you just can't beat our arts events, galleries, and museums, but particularly mentioned in the survey were The SC State Museum, Spoleto in Charleston, and ArtFields in Lake City.

*A few things people don't want to lose as we grow are the pace of life; the Southern culture, traditions and languages; our love of God and country; and the variety of people who live here.

*Speaking of culture and tradition, the question asked about what sport represents South Carolina was a no-brainer. More than 90% of the responses were: college football. No surprise there.

But hold on—we can't forget USC Women's Basketball, and how about those National Baseball champions at Coastal? They were all highly praised as well, as was golf. We have an estimated number of 478 golf courses throughout the state.

Hunting and fishing also topped the responses of favorite and traditional past times. Some of the best of both are found right here in our lakes, rivers, and streams.

*All respondents mentioned treasured and lasting images of South Carolina: views of the Appalachian foothills, acres of sandhill pines, stretches of white sand beaches, streets and roads with an ethereal quality created by the twisted limbs of live oaks and the almost Asian feel of the gnarled and blooming dogwoods. When asked what color they think of in terms of the state, the answers paint a portrait in greens, blues, purple, garnet, and yellows.

In looking over the collective answers, it is certainly obvious South Carolinians treasure their individual and collective heritages, acknowledge their shortcomings, and work toward making their home state a better and more beautiful place to live.

And despite our differences in politics, race, religion, education, profession, music, or taste preference in barbeque sauces, blooming throughout these stories about life here within her boundaries is an obvious sense of kinship with one another, generation to generation, rooted in shared love for our beloved state.

County Fare

South Carolina's 46 Counties are home to any number of fascinating historical, cultural, and unusual events and sights. Read below for 'just a taste' of what can be discovered and enjoyed here in our state.

Counties each have websites that contain more in depth information about the events and places listed below.

Abbeville County: Don't miss the Abbeville Spring Festival that offers an antique car show, music, great food, and rides for the youngsters. In autumn, good food, music, and dancing is available at the Due West Fall Festival.

Aiken County: The town of Aiken was voted Southern Living Magazine's Best Small Town in the South 2018. Aiken is home to The Thoroughbred Racing Hall of Fame. Aiken horse trainers trained the champion thoroughbred flat racers and steeplechase horses featured there.

For even more fun, visitors can attend The Southern City Film Festival (SCFF) to screen films, rub elbows with celebrities in the business, win prizes, and attend VIP parties.

Aiken also hosts the Chitlin' Strut each year featuring a hog calling contest, a strut dancing contest, and boiled and fried chitlins (if you dare). Join in a hawg-calling contest and admire the crowning of the Chitlin' Queens.

Keep an eye-out for Big Foot while traveling through the county. He has been known to wander in South Carolina. On January 15, 2015, Aiken welcomed researchers in the Animal Planet's "Finding Bigfoot" society who visited to seek proof of Big Foot's existence in SC.

Allendale County: Formed in 1919, Allendale is the youngest county in SC. Red Bluff Flint Quarries in Allendale County is an historic archeological site of outcrops of flint which in prehistoric times was used by Native Americans for raw material for tools.

The Allendale County Cooter Fest attracts thousands of visitors each year to its carnival, cooter- turtle races, games, street dances, live music, and great food.

Anderson County: The municipality of Anderson is known as the "Electric City" because it was the South's first city to use long distance cables to carry electricity generated from hydroelectric power plants. The county's Palmetto Moonshine is the first legal moonshine distillery in SC and sits across the street from the Anderson Courthouse. Not to be missed is the Carolina Brew-ha-Ha where offerings of both nationally and locally brewed beers are served. The festival has become so popular that Olly Smith, host of Travel Channel UK's "Ale Trails," filmed a segment of the festival in 2017.

Visitors also enjoy the Jockey Lot located in Anderson, one of the biggest flea markets in the United States, and each year crowds of people attend the annual honey-sopping contest at the Sugarfoot Festival in Honea Path.

And if "big" matters, The Bass Master Classic, called by many "The Super Bowl of Bass Tournament Fishing," is the place to be. The 2018 tournament will pay out $1,000,000 in prize money to the 52 contestants, with a $300,000 prize going to the winner.

In addition, people and hot air balloons descend on Anderson each year for the annual Hot Air Balloon Festival, an exciting and colorful event against the South Carolina blue skies.

Not to be missed: The Pendleton District Agricultural Museum displays the FIRST boll weevil found in SC. (He's a crispy critter by now, for sure.)

Bamberg County: On January 15, 1915, the small Denmark office of American Telephone and Telegraph Company in Bamberg County took part in the first historic transcontinental telephone call on Jan. 15, 1915.

The town of Denmark hosts the annual Dogwood Festival featuring arts, crafts, music, rides for the children, and food.

Barnwell County: Barnwell's courthouse lawn features a unique vertical sundial, a gift to the town in 1858 by Joseph D. Allen, who was a state Senator from Barnwell at the time. Legend has it that this is the only vertical sundial in the United States. The sundial keeps within two minutes of standard time even though it was erected before that time measure came into effect.

Also, the waters from God's Acre Healing spring in Barnwell are said to heal the sick. The former owner of the spring deeded it to God

Beaufort County: Dr. Martin Luther King, Jr. often secretly visited the Penn Center located on St. Helena Island in Beaufort County. Early drafts of parts of his famous "I Have a Dream" speech were actually penned in Gantt Cottage where he stayed there.

Hilton Head Island in Beaufort Country was voted Southern Living Magazine's Best Beach in the South 2018. Hilton Head offers exquisite beaches, some of the best seafood around, and boutique shopping to its visitors.

Bluffton, just minutes from Hilton Head, invites visitors to "go nuts" with them at the annual Bluffton Boiled Peanut Festival. Visitors enjoy a boiled peanut eating contest, a Peanut Costume Pageant, and can attend the Lil' Miss Peanut, Lil' Mr Goober, and Lil' Baby Goober Pageants.

On Morgan Island, just off the coast of South Carolina, live an estimated 3500 monkeys—thus the local name: Monkey Island. They are the only free-ranging monkeys in the US.

Berkeley County: Hell-Hole Swamp located in Jamestown, SC, features an annual festival where visitors can participate in the tobacco-spitting contest and a legs contest, as well as the 10K Hell Hole Gater Trot (also known as the "Redneck Run.") It is the oldest 10K in the Low Country, beating our Charleston's Cooper River Bridge Run.

Local legend tells of how General Cornwallis named the swamp in a letter he wrote to King George claiming General Marion and his soldiers eluded him by simply disappearing into "one hell-hole of a swamp."

Moncks Corner offers Shucking in the Park each year where visitors can eat their fill of oysters, and St. Stephen's Catfish Festival features the treat of catfish and the Sweet Pea Contest. Both have music and entertainment for the family.

Calhoun County: Named for former U.S. Vice-President John C. Calhoun, Calhoun County is located in the Black Belt section of the state known in former years for its many plantations. The term originally referred to the dark, fertile soil that was indicative of a swath of land throughout the Southeast.

The Honey Jubilee and Farm Fest held in St. Matthews not only offers great food, music, and fun to its visitors, but also it offers an educational opportunity to learn more about bees and their importance to humans.

Charleston County: The city of Charleston was voted America's #1 Small City, five years and counting and voted Southern Living Magazine's Best City in the South 2018.

Throughout the county historical sites abound. Take a carriage ride, visit the beaches and barrier islands, and eat scrumptious delicacies at any one of the many restaurants throughout the county.

The city of Charleston and the surrounding islands and smaller towns feature a number of festivals each year and each season. Among them are the internationally known Spoleto Arts Festival and the Charleston Wine and Food festival. In addition, visitors might attend the Charleston Film Festival and the Low Country Oyster Festival. More locally, guest may discover the Hat Ladies Easter Promenade where participants don their

Easter bonnets and finery and stroll down Broad Street—a special treat at Easter and a herald of spring.

Cherokee County: Cherokee lays claim to beautiful King's Mountain National Military State Park where the battle of Kings Mountain was fought October 7th, 1780. This was an important American victory during the Revolutionary War. The battle was the first major patriot victory to occur after the British invasion of Charleston, SC, in May 1780.

The town of Gaffney hosts the SC Peach Festival where visitors enjoy competing in the peach eating contest and the dessert eating contest. Later, they can watch the Peach Parade, enjoy the music, browse the car show, or enjoy the mud bog.

Chester County: Chester invites guests to check out the Haunted Hill Motel located in Great Falls and stay at the beautiful Inn on York Street. The town hosts Hog on the Hill every year where attendees sample fare from the contestants in the cook off and later enjoy a picnic on the grounds.

Great Falls is the home of the Flopeye Fish Festival which includes a carnival, arts and crafts, and a car show.

Chesterfield County: This county is located in the Sandhills State Forest. There are events on the 47,850 acres of forest year round from bird watching to dog trials. Sugarloaf Mountain is also a part of the State Forest. "The Mountain" is an unusual geological phenomenon towering 100 feet above the surrounding terrain.

Several festivals are held annually: The Cheraw Spring Festival offers good food, music, and entertainment for the family; Pageland hosts the nationally-renowned Watermelon Festival; Patrick's Pine Straw Festival celebrates long-leaf pine straw and includes the Taste of Patrick for visitors; Jefferson offers the Blue Jay Festival and lots of family fun, and guests can "experience the joy of jazz" from "the head to the toes" at Cheraw's Jazz Festival in the fall.

Clarendon County: This county boasts one of the largest man-made lakes in the United States, Lake Marion,_which was completed in 1941 as a New Deal_project. Each year, the Manning community celebrates all that "the lake" offers at The Striped Bass Festival with food, pageants, music, and games for all.

Turbeville claims The Puddin' Swamp Festival as its own offering a corn hole tournament, music, food, and entertainment as well as the Miss Swamp Bottom Beauty Contest.

Colleton County: Walterboro takes pride in their low country beauty, where visitors gravitate to The Artisan's Center or can travel a little farther into the rural area of the county to quiet, beautiful Edisto Beach.

Walterboro also hosts the Rice Festival where visitors enjoy music, arts, crafts, and a corn hole tournament.

Darlington County: As home to the Darlington Raceway, which hosts the annual NASCAR Southern 500 Darlington also offers visitors an opportunity to "Experience the Richard Petty Driving Experience!"

Meanwhile, Scarlett's Antiques in the town of Darlington offers a change of pace and some beautiful bargains. Lamar, SC, in Darlington County, sponsors the Egg Scramble Jamboree with a beauty pageant, carnival rides and a night parade.

Dillon County: The Little Pee Dee State Park which offers fishing, camping and picnicking is one of the highlights of the county. Dillon County is also home to the South of the Border, a resort and major tourist attraction located on I-95 at the NC state line. Children love the billboard signs along the interstate that promote South of the Border and all its attractions. Check out their new reptile lagoon.

Dorchester County: This county offers a smorgasbord of things to choose from: Frankie's Fun Park, Middleton Place tours, Oakbrook Nature Trail, just to name a few.

Summerville, SC, is the birthplace of sweet tea, the state's hospitality beverage, and the home of the "Sweet Tea Trail." As a side note, Wadmallaw Island lays claim to being the only tea plantation in the United States and named its brand "American Classic Tea." Summerville lies within Dorchester (mainly), Berkeley, and Charleston Counties.

Not far from Summerville, the town of St. George holds the annual World Grits Festival where visitors can roll in a giant vat of grits.

Edgefield County: Downtown Edgefield boasts the Carolina Moon Distillery where guests can sample a variety of moonshines and mixed drinks. And don't skip a taste of the Rabbit's Spit.

Johnston, SC, lays claim to the honor of "Peach Capital of the World."

Visitors interested in wildlife should head over to the National Wild Turkey Federation Wild Turkey Center for all the scoop on turkey history and turkey preservation in South Carolina. See the world's largest turkey call, animatronic sculptures, lots of exhibits, and try-out the laser firing range.

Fairfield County: The town of Fairfield offers choices of an historic tour or a Murder & Mayhem tour among other attractions.

Ridgeway is home to the smallest police station in the world. It is actually a toll booth and was in full use from 1940-1990 (Jarvis).

The South Carolina Railroad Museum in Winnsboro offers train rides and a gift shop that sells train sets, among other things, and Lake Wateree State Park is just a short drive from Winnsboro.

Florence County: Quiet Lake City is home to one of the two largest tobacco markets in the state. The town is also host of Artfields, an impressive, serious arts festival held each year in the spring.

The town of Florence offers great shopping and a variety of restaurants, among its other attractions, and tiny Turbeville sponsors the Puddin' Swamp Festival each year. Visitors enjoy the Miss Swamp Bottom Beauty Contest, a corn hole contest, and a fireworks display.

Georgetown County: Georgetown and Horry County share the quiet community at Murrell's Inlet, the home to world famous Brookgreen Gardens, the largest collection of outdoor sculpture in the country. Murrell's Inlet also hosts Shag Fest and sponsors the Blessing of the Inlet Sound each year.

Just down the road, Pawley's Island, which many native South Carolinians claim is the best kept coastal secret in the state, boasts beautiful beaches, the Turtle Strut 5K and 8K, and a host of good eatin' places along Highway 17. Many of the island residents are members of South Carolina United Turtle Enthusiasts (S.C.U.T.E.) Visitors can often catch a tour or casual informative gatherings on the beach to learn about the protected turtles.

Greenville County: This upstate county sponsors a number of fun festivals. The city of Greenville hosts the Blues Festival each year and Artisphere; while, nearby Mauldin lays claim to the Sooie Festival (pronounced SUE-EEE).

Tiny Greer has the Spring Skunk Music Festival; and Fountain Inn claims dibs on the Cornbread and Collard Greens Festival where guests enjoy music, food, and fun.

Greenwood County: Greenwood has an Aviation Expo and the nationally recognized SC Festival of Flowers where guests are invited to have a "bloomin' good time" and admire an array of brilliantly colored blossoms.

Hampton County: Yemassee holds its annual Shrimp Festival in September. There is also a Watermelon Festival where attendees enjoy music, food, and a Tractor Operating Contest.

Also gracing the county are the beautiful ruins of Old Sheldon Church—a "must not" miss site for those interested in history and architecture.

Horry County: Harvest Hoe-Down Festival is held in Aynor, and Little River hosts a Shrimp Fest with music and the best seafood available.

Myrtle Beach, long a tourist attraction, offers endless dining and entertainment venues, beautiful beaches and the Sun Fun Festival each year. Myrtle Beach is also said to be the birthplace of the state dance: The Shag.

Jasper County: This county lies in the southern-most portion of the state. In Hardeeville, (part of which lies in Beaufort County) visitors can join in the fun each year at the SC/GA Barbeque Festival. The town is also known as the home of two life-sized elephants, one pink and one gray, that grace the entrance to a fireworks store there.

Sergeant Jasper Park is a short drive away.

Kershaw County: Famous for the annual Carolina Cup, a steeple chase horse racing event, Camden is the site of one of South Carolina's rites of spring. Whether or not visitors attend because of the races, the socializing, alone, offers sights of "most anythin' you can think of." The ladies hats and the food are two of the most compelling examples of what attendees enjoy.

The tiny town of Boykin holds an annual Christmas parade where participants make, build, borrow, or invent their own parade floats, caravans, rides, marches, or dances. Most anything that can be "ridden or driven" finds a place in the parade. The gathering features music, fun, and lots of tailgating delicacies.

The state's dog also calls Boykin home. In the 1900's, L.W. 'Whit' Boykin bred the curly-haired, brown dog dubbed the Boykin Spaniel.

Lancaster County: This county secured its place in history as the home of the seventh President of the United States, Andrew Jackson. Visitors can visit the Andrew Jackson State Park there.

Guests to the area can tour the Native American Studies Center dedicated to the Catawba Native Americans. The Center provides an educational and fun experience for visitors of all ages.

Also intriguing is Bob Doster's Artist Studio/Gallery/Sculpture Garden. Doster's sculptures in stainless is praised world-wide as some of the finest.

Laurens County: Laurens shares the town of Fountain Inn with Greenville County. Fountain Inn proclaims it is the home to Clayton "peg leg" Bates, a famous dancer. At twelve, Bates lost a leg in a cotton gin accident, but eventually became a famous dancer who performed more than 20 times on the Ed Sullivan Show. His famous, signature step was the "Imitation American Jet Plane" in which he jumped up to five feet in the air and then landed on his "peg leg" with his "good leg" straight behind him.

Lee County: Dalton Stevens of Bishopville attached buttons to just about everything including clothes and a hearse. Stop by to see his Button Museum. Sharing top billing for area attractions are the gardens of Pearl Frye who creates sculptures from trees, plants, and also creates works from found objects.

Beware! There may be a Lizard Man roaming dark roads and bridges at night in Lee County.

Lexington County: The town of Lexington claims the honor of making the largest tires in the world. The tires are called "Earthmover" tires and are 14 feet across.

The county is also host to the Okra Strut Festival where visitors participate in and enjoy (or not) an okra-eating contest.

And don't feed Messie if you happen to come across her in Lake Murray. Unlike her first cousin Nessie the Loch Ness Monster, Messie is said to be a bit aggressive.

Marion County: The town of Mullins garnered fame as the Tobacco Capital of SC after the tobacco plants arrived in the area in 1894, creating a wave of building throughout the county—500 tobacco barns. The first sale of tobacco was held in August 28, 1895.

Marion is also the site for the annual Foxtrot Festival. The term foxtrot doesn't refer to the dance, although there is dancing at the festival. Instead, the name references the SC Revolutionary War Hero General Francis Marion known as the Swamp Fox.

Marion also claims if you drink the waters of Catfish Creek, you will fall in love with the area and never leave.

Marlboro County: This county was home to the Pee Dee Indian Tribe. The county seat courthouse was spared in Sherman's burnings across the state and contains one of South Carolina's oldest complete set of county records.

A long-told legend claims land in Marlboro County was so rich and fertile, people purchased it by the pound rather than by the acre.

McCormick County: Heritage Gold Mine Park offers visitors the unique experience of panning for gold and also gem screening. Children and adults both enjoy this adventure.

Also of interest is Dorn's Flour and Grist Mill, which was originally built as a cotton gin that ran by steam.

The Bells and Whistles Festival draws hundreds of visitors each year to celebrate all things "bells and whistles" at the SC Wild's Heritage Center.

Newberry County: The town of Newberry sponsors Pork in the Park each year, a sanctioned competition by the Southern BBQ Network.

The county is also the home of ancient Indian sites, battlefields, the Quaker Cemetery and beautiful Lynches Woods. An amazing scenic road runs through the forest. Visitors might also tour the Japanese Gardens and Enoree River Winery.

Oconee County: Known as the "Golden Corner" of the state, Oconee County touts their ideal climate, beautiful lakes, and awe-inspiring mountains as the best anywhere. Guests have access to three parks: Chau Ram Park, High Falls Park, and South Cove Park where they can enjoy hiking, camping, and fishing. (Chaw Ram Park is known as the best kept secret of the area. Visit it to find out why.)

Orangeburg County: The beautiful Edisto Memorial Gardens in Orangeburg (known as the "Garden City") is home to award winning All-American Rose Selections. And yes, the Festival of Roses is an annual event.

There is also a Raylrode Daze Festival in Branchville featuring music, dancing, a pet show, and a talent show along with the traditional beauty pageant and parade.

Springfield's annual Governor's Frog Jumping and Egg Striking Contest is held every Easter weekend (52 years and counting). The festival is modeled after the famous frog jumping contest in Mark Twain's "The Celebrated Jumping Frog of Calaveras County." The winner in the contest takes home a $750 prize...not pulling any "legs" here, folks.

And for those who like something a little other-worldly, check out the Welcome Center built by Jody Pendarvis of Bowman for aliens, if and when they land here.

Pickens County: This county offers impressive hiking trails and waterfalls. Visitors will enjoy Twin Falls in the Eatatoe Valley and Table Rock State Park.

There's fun to be had at the "Pickin' in Pickens," as well. Other events include the Founders Day Festival, the Azalea Festival, and the Blue Ridge Festival, which is a premier charity event each year offering music, food, classic cars, and other entertainment.

Richland County: It is difficult to run out of places to visit and things to do in Richland County. Visit any number of historical sites throughout the area. Dine at the drool-worthy restaurants. Stroll Riverbanks Zoo, the State Museum, and numerous art galleries. Or visitors can escape to the countryside by traveling to the little town of Hopkins and walking the trails of the beautiful Congaree National Forest.

And don't miss the more than 2000 animals homed without bars or cages in naturalized habitats at the Riverbanks Zoological Park in Columbia. Top notch!

Saluda County: Near Richland Creek stands the Bonham House, which marks the birthplace of Alamo hero James Butler Bonham. The county calls itself "the place where Texas was born." Aside from the Saluda County Museum, visitors also enjoy touring the four nostalgic bridges in the area.

Campbell's Covered Bridge is built of pine. It puts visitors in mind of painted landscapes of years ago.

Klickety-Klack Bridge is the handiwork of two guys (Don Spann and Troy Coffey) plus a tractor named "Old Blue." Spann set the floor timbers of the bridge in a pattern that makes a "klickety-klack" sound when a car crosses over them, thus the name of the bridge.

Ballenger's Covered Bridge is privately owned. The wooden bridge has a tin roof and spans a southern portion of the Middle Tyger River. Visitors are welcome to drive through the picturesque property and cross the bridge.

The fourth bridge is the oldest bridge in SC, the historic Poinsett Bridge. It was constructed in 1820 of locally quarried stone and features stepped, parapet sidewalls with a Gothic arch 15-feet over Little Gap Creek. It served as one of three bridges on a toll road running from Charleston to Asheville, N.C.

Spartanburg County: The town of Spartanburg is the sight of the oldest stadium in the nation for minor league players: Duncan Park Baseball Stadium.

The County hosts a Stone Soup Storytelling Festival in Woodruff each year, as well as hosting "Spartanburg Soaring" where professional kite flyers demonstrate the art.

Campobello, SC has the Plum Hollow Festival and promotes its Bootlegger's Ball as a main attraction.

The county is also home to a Moonshiners Reunion and a Mountain Music Festival.

Sumter County: The county boasts the largest gingko farm in the world. The town of Sumter is also home to the world renowned Swan Lake Iris Gardens, the only public park in the United States to home all eight species of swans. Visitors also wander through some of the most beautiful and extensive displays of Japanese iris. During the Swan Lake Iris Festival, visitors enjoy music, food, and arts and crafts. And in the Christmas Season, Swan Lake Gardens wraps itself in sparkling colored lights for the Fantasy of Lights and stays open into the evening for visitors to enjoy the sight.

South Carolina has an official waltz which is actually a song, not a dance. From over three hundred years ago, it passed down by ear through the Richardson family in Sumter county from which several governors descended.

The Bradford family of Sumter has been growing a South Carolina variety of watermelons for more than 170 years. The melon is named the Bradford melon, naturally.

The little town of Rembert goes western at the Black Cowboy Festival offering hay rides, western dance, and horse competitions.

Shaw Air Force Base is also one of Sumter County's prides. As one of the largest military bases operated by the United States, Shaw is one of only two air bases in CONUS that has an active railroad line. In 2011, as a result of military base consolidations across the county, Third Army Headquarters moved to Shaw, as well. Both the air force and the army personnel and their families provide strong support for the community as well as for the nation.

Union County: This section of the state served as a huge hunting territory for the Cherokee Indians before white settlers came to the region.

Visitors can tour The Piedmont Physic Garden, a nonprofit botanical garden where many plants containing historical medicinal uses are grown. Some of the plants are native to the Piedmont and Southern Appalachian areas. The garden serves as a link between people and the world of plants and to educate them on the importance of plants in daily life.

New to the area is the Union County Dragway, a motorsport park featuring America's largest off-road motorcycle and ATV racing series.

Williamsburg County: As home to Moore Farms Botanical Garden, 65 acres of cultivated gardens and pastoral fields are located in Lake City. Visitors can tour the grounds and explore the buildings.

Wee Tee Wildlife Management Area is also homed in Williamsburg. It is a natural area for wildlife observation, as well as for hunting and fishing.

York County: The town of Smyrna holds title to the smallest of SC towns. It is only .7 square miles and home to 45 people. The town, small as it is, lies in both York and Cherokee Counties.

Rock Hill is the largest town in York County and is the site of a Spring Festival held in beautiful Glencairn Garden.

Visitors should check out the Children's Museum and Canaan Zipline Canopy Tour.

Warning! Beware the Carolina Reaper Pepper, the world's hottest chili pepper according to the Guiness World Records. Smokin' Ed Currie, proprietor of the PuckerButt Pepper Company in Fort Mill, SC, bred the pepper in Rock Hill.

Y'all come see us!

95755225R00169

Made in the USA
Columbia, SC
16 May 2018